ONE FLESH

A PRACTICAL GUIDE
TO HONEYMOON SEX
AND BEYOND

AMELIA & GREG CLARKE

ONE FLESH

A PRACTICAL GUIDE TO HONEYMOON SEX AND BEYOND

AMELIA & GREG CLARKE

 matthiasmedia

SYDNEY · YOUNGSTOWN

Matthias Media
(St Matthias Press Ltd ACN 067 558 365)
Email: info@matthiasmedia.com.au
Internet: www.matthiasmedia.com.au
Please visit our website for current postal and telephone
contact information.

Matthias Media (USA)
Email: sales@matthiasmedia.com
Internet: www.matthiasmedia.com
Please visit our website for current postal and telephone
contact information.

ISBN 978 1 925424 34 8

Cover design and typesetting by Lankshear Design.

Contents

Dear Reader

This book is written for two kinds of readers. The first kind is the Christian couple that is about to get married. They would like some advice on what is about to happen between them, and some ideas from those who have gone before about how to begin a happy and fruitful sexual life together. We hope that this book is just the introduction required. Without going into too much detail, it provides information on what to expect of your sexual relationship, how to get started in a way that is pleasing for both the husband and wife, and how to establish patterns and behaviours that will help you to enhance your sexual relationship throughout a long marriage.

This first kind of reader may be surprised by some of the book's content, because we have tried also to be realistic about what can go wrong between a couple in the sexual arena: common physical problems, the impact of sexual 'baggage' which is brought into the relationship, and the possible effects of sexual sin. We encourage engaged couples and newlyweds to read this material as an investment in your life together. For some, it will be difficult material to read. But we hope that it all becomes armour against the various assaults that will be made upon your marriage over time.

The second kind of reader has been married for a bit longer, but has always wondered whether their sexual relationship is going in a healthy direction. This book spells out the kinds of things that often get in the road of a godly and happy sex life. We hope that for some of these readers the book introduces them to the honeymoon they never had.

Because we want people actually to read this book before they marry, and not just to leave it unticked at the foot of a long 'To Do Before The Wedding' list, the book is necessarily introductory. Each of the areas we discuss could be given much longer and more detailed treatment, and we offer recommendations of other books which can provide this for the interested and less time-pressured person or couple. We don't cover differences resulting from racial and religious upbringing, nor questions of cultural behaviour, nor do we consider the effects of prolonged or chronic illness on a couple's relationship. These may be important to you, and there are other books that can provide more details.

This is a book written for Christians, and written with the belief that the Bible offers guidance for us about how to live in order to please God in a world that is tainted by human sinfulness. We have, however, made use of research and thinking outside of the Christian world where appropriate, and hope that readers will see the value in doing this. For anyone who isn't a Christian and happens to read this book, we hope and pray that it recommends the Christian faith to you, for the way of life and the relationship with God that is available through Jesus Christ has no match—not even in the most fulfilling of marriages.

To respond to anything written in this book, or to make other enquiries, send an email to: oneflesh@matthiasmedia.com.au

Great expectations

David and Sandra Keller fell back on their pillows, exhausted, spent, and happy as heaven. Sandra's head rested on David's chest, her gentle breath on his skin a sign of her contentment. David was beaming from ear to ear, his face aglow with pride, and with love. They were married; they were one flesh. They had just enjoyed sex for the first time, and it was exactly as the movies had shown them.

Arriving in their fifteenth floor hotel room after a fabulous wedding and reception, David had swept his new wife into his arms, shouldered open the door with masculine ease, and transported her to the edge of the gorgeous four-poster bed. He had knelt in front of her, kissing her hands, her arms, her neck, her shoulders. Slowly, skilfully, he had removed her beautiful 'going away' dress. It slid to the floor like a silken skin she was shedding.

For the next two hours, they had caressed, embraced, cried and laughed, until they were both in a heightened state of love and excitement. Sandra had touched David just as he liked to be touched—he had never felt so alive; and he had known how to arouse her at just the right pace—slow, but not too slow, eager but never too eager.

When he finally entered her, and they consummated their love, they felt as if their whole world was perfect. They loved each other like this until they both could last no longer, whereupon they raced to a summit and threw themselves off, two bodies as one, into the sexual ecstasy of orgasm.

In the afterglow, they both shook their heads in delight at the wonder of marriage and the joy of first-time sex.

Donald and Sarah Koo were turned away from each other in the bed, facing the opposite walls of their honeymoon suite. Sarah was weeping quietly, while Donald fought back words of anger, and tried to deal with his intense, unspent, sexual desire.

Arriving in their fifteenth floor hotel room after a disappointing wedding service (yes, the best man did forget the ring; and it had been raining so Sarah's dress was damaged), and a long evening reception during which Sarah's mother had virtually ignored her, they walked awkwardly through the honeymoon suite door. On the drive from the reception centre, Sarah had been telling Donald everything that went wrong during the service. She was very stressed and tired. Donald had tried to soothe her for the first ten minutes, but then he just went quiet. He wondered whether she would feel better after a long shower with him.

When they were in the room, Sarah threw herself on the bed and started crying. Donald knelt next to her and patted her back, wondering what to do next. Before he knew it, he was stroking her neck and then her breasts. She rolled away and shoved her face into a pillow. "Not yet!" she called out in a muffled yell. Donald was a little shocked, but he withdrew, and suggested that they talk for a while.

"OK, OK", Sarah said through sniffles, and sat up on the bed. They talked for an hour, Sarah crying and Donald trying to soothe her, but getting nowhere. He started to feel angry and hurt—this was supposed to be their wedding night! He decided to try to move things towards sex: he stroked her breast again. Her reaction shocked him. She gave him a withering stare, rose to her feet and ran into the bathroom where she closed and locked the door. And continued crying.

Sarah stayed in the bathroom for one and a half hours, despite Donald's pleading that she come out. Eventually, he told her he was going to sleep and climbed into bed. When Sarah emerged, she was still in her wedding dress, with its water stains. She climbed into the other side of the bed, and they lay there with their eyes open and their hearts breaking.

Dmitri and Soula Kristos rested their heads together on the pillow. There was a soberness to their mood, despite it being their wedding night. "I don't think I should have invited Paul", Soula murmured.

"It was fine", Dmitri replied unconvincingly.

"He had no right saying what he said on our wedding day. He has never, never, been able to accept that it's over", said Soula.

"Well, it's well and truly over, isn't it", said Dmitri. "He should have worked that out today."

"You're a good man, Dmitri", said Soula, searching her husband's face with her eyes, and trying to convey her complete devotion to him.

"Mmm", was all Dmitri could manage. He sighed, and stroked her hair.

Arriving in their fifteenth floor hotel room, they had held hands as Dmitri turned the key. The room was nice, familiar, reminiscent of many things for both of them—some of them memories they shared, some of them not. They ran a bath, undressed together quickly, and jumped in. They sat comfortably with each other for a while, before scrubbing each other's backs, washing their hair, and then cracking open the champagne.

It was very enjoyable, very comfortable, almost as if they had been married for years. After the bath, Soula phoned her mum to tell her how the room was, and what time the plane left in the morning. They chatted for about half an hour while Dmitri reclined on the bed and watched some sport on television.

Soula got off the phone and hopped into bed. Tired, but happy, they began to stroke each other and enjoy the familiar sex they had learned with each other over the past year.

Dan and Samantha Ketchen slept next to each other, not quite peacefully, not quite happily. It was late, and they had had a long day, having driven from the reception centre in the neighbouring state to this idyllic hotel they had both always dreamed of staying in.

Arriving in their fifteenth floor hotel room, Dan had carried a giggling Samantha into the room, where he had organized for her favourite flowers to be waiting beside the bed. She was elated, and she kissed him deeply and they hugged while standing for about ten minutes.

Dan then suggested gently, "Shall we lie down?" Samantha gave him a nervous look, but happily lowered herself back onto the bed, with Dan on top of her. There, they kissed and kissed, and stroked and caressed for a while. At that point, Dan undid his zipper, reached under Samantha's dress and removed her pants, and tried to enter her.

Samantha let out a yelp.

"What, what, what!" Dan blurted out, anxious and sexually overwhelmed all at once.

"Ca- can you wait?" Samantha asked with a furrowed brow.

"Er, what do you mean? Um. No. Oh! Sorry. Too late."

"Oh", said Samantha, as he fell to the bed beside her.

They cuddled, Samantha said it was OK, and they started chatting about the wedding. But after a few minutes, Samantha noticed that she was talking to herself. She pulled the sheets over them both, and joined her new husband in sleep.

The wedding night is one of the holy grails of life, the time when fantasy and reality are supposed to meet, when a man and woman find the ultimate union for which they have been longing, planning and imagining. If you have been there, you may have recognized one of the above scenarios. If you are thinking of being there in the near future, you may be hoping to be David and Sandra, but worrying that you will be one of the other 'D' and 'S's. Or you may be thinking, "Of course we'll be David and Sandra. What could possibly stand in our way?"

This book is written both to help couples have a better chance of having something which even approximates the David and Sandra experience on their wedding night and on into married life together. But it is also written with the realization that the David and Sandra experience is *always a thing of fiction* and bears no relation to the way most couples begin married life together, let alone the way they continue through years of marriage. We hope to provide the best possible information on sex and marriage for engaged couples, newlyweds, and those who may have been married for a while but need to go back and think about their relationship afresh.

It's everywhere and nowhere

We've seen sex used to sell ice cream. For some reason, it sells cars. It also sells electronic gadgetry, judging by the nubile women draping the covers of technology magazines in newsagents around the country. Of course, there is an abundance of pornography sitting on the shelves, but there are also the 'women's magazines', their headlines promising more sex, more orgasmic sex, more frequent sex, less frequent but more satisfying sex, longer and slower sex, faster sex, sex with multiple partners, and sex with one partner multiple times.

Yet despite the public prominence of sex, actual discussion of sexual matters between couples, friends or family is quite rare. It is as if the torrent of material on sex in the media silences discussion. Do we feel that we are meant to know about it all already? Do we feel we will look naïve if we have to talk about it?

It is even rarer among Christians. It is as if we have reacted against the public outpourings on sex by making it an off-limits discussion in churches and youth groups and Bible study gatherings. This is a great shame, for the Bible gives a significant amount of space to discussions of sex, and the advice it has to give us is second to none. It is more realistic and practical than many Christians realize.

We need to recover ways of talking about sex that are appropriate to different situations. This book deals with the discussion of the topic between husband and wife, with brief forays into how you might talk about problems with a friend, professional or pastor. However, Christians also need to rediscover appropriate ways of discussing the subject in youth groups (even in Sunday Schools, given the current low age of sexual awareness), in small groups (where there is opportunity to help each other with individual issues), and among couples who have been married for some time (when patterns of sexual behaviour have become ingrained, and it is awkward and complicated to make changes). We hope to deal with some of these topics in future publications.

Much of this book is about learning to talk about sex. It also contains practical information on starting out in a sexual relationship within marriage, but the heart of the book is its plea that couples *communicate* on this very intimate topic. Openness, honesty, realism and pleasurable conversation will ensure that your relationship grows, regardless of any sexual problems that might arise. A healthy sexual conversation between spouses is a form of protection for the relationship. It helps you to withstand the difficulties and different phases of married life. It's what marriage is all about. "Marriage is one long conversation, chequered by disputes", wrote Robert Louis Stevenson. Our hope is that the disputes will be carried out in love and will lead to a better understanding of each other, and that the conversation will always seem too short.

Good, godly sex

Good sex doesn't just happen. Neither does godly sex. For both to occur, education is required. For both to occur, commitment is required. Godly sex occurs when a couple understands the teaching of the Scriptures on the subject of sex in marriage, and obeys that teaching. Good sex occurs when godly sex is combined with a proper understanding of the physical and emotional sides of sex.

In Part I, we briefly examine the Bible's teaching on sex, focusing primarily on how it affects a couple who are preparing for marriage. However, what is said is relevant no matter how long a couple has been married, since the biblical ideal is that marriage lasts for a lifetime.

In Parts II and III, we consider the physical, emotional and relational aspects of sex. How does a couple get to know each other's bodies, each other's sexual anxieties, each other's sexual delights? We provide a 'honeymoon pack' of practical information on how to enjoy the first sexual experiences of marriage, as well as outlining the pitfalls to avoid and how to prepare for what can commonly go wrong.

In Part IV, we quickly cover the most common and most serious sexual problems that can occur between a couple, focusing mainly on the major medical problems. This section is necessarily introductory, and will not provide all the information required on subjects such as homosexuality, sexual abuse and other serious circumstances. However, it will point you in the right direction if these are issues facing you as a couple.

Throughout the book, we have interwoven stories related to the subjects being discussed. These are imaginary stories, although they can easily be drawn from life, and any counsellor in this area will have seen plenty of cases that match the stories we have told. We would like to emphasize again that these are not actual case histories, but common scenarios which help to put flesh on the bones of the ideas we cover in the main text.

We have also provided, here and there, random observations and ideas for reflection, under the title of 'Pillow Talk'. These are occasionally controversial, occasionally 'obvious and straightforward'; either way, we hope they lead to many fruitful

Part I

Understanding sex from a Christian perspective

Part 1

utside Christianity, and sometimes inside it, there is a view that God doesn't like sex. If there is one thing that the Church is against, it is sex. Some people think that Adam and Eve's sin in the Garden of Eden was to have sex, and the apple has become a symbol of stolen love—the forbidden fruit.

The forbidden fruit isn't sex. Let us say upfront that sex is one of God's good gifts to a man and woman. It is the celebration of the body, in its physical pleasures and its marvellous capacity to bring about heightened states of enjoyment. It is the celebration of the bonding of two people, making them as one, in an earthy yet mysterious act which is so obviously more than just two bodies connecting. Sex is an emotional rollercoaster, offering highs and lows, depending on the relationship between the two people involved.

There is also a view that says the Christian attitude to sex is very restrictive. Christians are those for whom sex must always mean "lights off, no talking, man on top, do the task at hand". Jokes about Christians only having sex in the 'missionary' position are common. Even among Christians themselves, there can be resistance to the idea that sex is a rich and varied experience of intimate physical and emotional bonding between a husband and wife. Sometimes we live up to the jokes that are made about us.

Christians rightly emphasize that sex is not a joking matter. We grant a high degree of importance to sex, and want to be sure that we are doing things God's way rather than just following our own desires. We know that God has communicated particular truths about sex in the Scriptures, and we are keen to make sure that we obey him. This godly impulse sometimes gets skewed into thinking that *any* discussion about sex—how to do it, variety in sexual positions, how to make it more enjoyable—borders on giving in to the lusts of the flesh. In order to avoid "foolish talk or coarse joking" (Eph 5:4) and to rein in passions that might lurch out of control, Christians can become silent on the topic of sex—even with their spouses.

This is a dangerous situation, and not one which encourages a good and godly sexual relationship between a couple. Sex requires words, if it is going to fulfil its created intentions. Fortunately, the Bible itself gives us a language of sex which can help us in discussions with our spouses. It depicts in detailed, often picturesque and exuberant language, the way in which a man and woman ought to relate sexually. It also spells out some of the consequences of sexual sin in enough detail to help us see why it is so harmful to a relationship. God's view of sex, as we discover it in the Bible, can be quite liberating as we find out how he made us. It can also be quite confronting, as we discover how far short of his goals we can fall.

Of course, the following brief survey of what the Bible says about sex doesn't contain everything that could be said. It's a quick look at the most important things.

Chapter 1

Sex in God's good creation

The Bible's first mention of sex is in the context of marriage. Its second mention refers to the birth of children. And its third refers to misplaced lust and its terrible consequences. These three ideas tell us a good deal about God's intentions with regards to sex.

In Genesis 2, Adam glories in the gift God has given him—a creature like no other, who is like him (in fact, created from his side), and in whom he delights. There is an air of exhilaration to Adam's statement: "This is now bone of my bones and flesh of my flesh" (Gen 2:23). The following verses spell out the power and the beauty of sex in marriage:

> **For this reason a man will leave his father and mother and be united to his wife, and they will become one flesh. The man and his wife were both naked, and they felt no shame. (Gen 2:24-25)**

Sex is a "one flesh" activity; it joins together two creatures of God who were, in fact, one at the beginning. Woman came from man, and is a part of man; sex maintains this unity, even though they are two separate beings. It is a wonderful two-in-oneness. This is a very lofty view of sex, and may even seem idealistic, romantic or fanciful to some of today's readers. But this is the teaching of Scripture: sex belongs to marriage between a man and a woman, who are considered as one flesh. There is no shame in it; rather, it is a cause for glory and exhilaration.

In the New Testament, this teaching is continued, as the husband is urged to love the body of his wife as if it were his own: "He who loves his wife loves himself" (Eph 5:28). This very close association of one's very own self with one's wife is extraordinarily important to understanding the place of sex in marriage. God's ideal is that a man and woman be united in marriage, and sex is an expression of that unity.

The next mention of sex in Genesis is Adam impregnating Eve with their son, Cain, and then his brother, Abel. Eve says, "With the help of the LORD I have brought forth a man" (Gen 4:1). This is a startling announcement which is easily overlooked: God the Creator enabled his creatures to bring forth life. The man and woman were enabled by God to create new life.

This reality always accompanies sex—children can result! Today's technologies give great control over this, but there is no such thing as foolproof contraception. Sex between a man and a woman always brings with it the possibility of pregnancy. A Christian couple needs to have this reality in mind when they begin their sexual relationship. It is not that they *must* be wanting to have children every time they have sex, or that using contraceptive measures is somehow ungodly. Rather, there needs to be acknowledgement that sex and begetting children (to use the old term) go together. This, too, is part of God's good provision for the couple, and for this reason there is often a prayer for "the blessing of children" in a Christian marriage ceremony.

Of course, the goodness of sex must be understood in light of the terrible truth of the human condition since the Fall: that goodness is now elusive. We still know what it is (thanks to the revelation of the Bible), but we find ourselves falling short of it over and over again. This is the sorry story which unfolds throughout the Bible, after Adam and Eve first fell into disobedience. In fact, the immediate motivation for the great Flood that destroyed the entire human race except the household of Noah, was sexual sin. This is reported in Genesis 6, in a story that is unusual to 21st century ears. The "sons of God", otherwise called the "Nephilim", married and slept with "the daughters of men", drawing judgment from God: "I am grieved that I have made them", are the horrific words he utters (Gen 6:7). This sin, no doubt among many other evil acts such as Cain murdering Abel in Genesis 4, led to the Flood. The improper lust of the Nephilim has dire consequences, as does all sexual sin.

But before we consider the consequences of sin in the fallen world, there are more positive teachings in the Scriptures which cannot be overlooked.

Sex is to be pleasurable

God created sex to be pleasurable. He gave us bodies capable of intense sexual arousal. He gave to the male immense excitement at the female form, at the scent of a woman, and at pretty much every aspect of female behaviour. To the woman, he gave a different kind of pleasure (we shall explore this difference later in the book), focused on the man's warmth towards her, his attentiveness, his talk of love—and his masculine body. Some say that the existence of the clitoris is testimony that God wants sex to be enjoyable. The clitoris performs no bodily function other than to provide sexual excitement for the woman. Its only role is to bring pleasure. Please don't think this irreverent or flippant—it says a good deal about the wonders of the human body as God has created it. God cares profoundly about our happiness, and one way he has demonstrated this is in making sex potentially pleasurable.

Much of the Bible book, Song of Songs, is concerned with the pleasures of sex. There is a focus on the many pleasurable elements of sex.

The sensual:

> My lover is to me a sachet of myrrh
>   resting between my breasts.
> My lover is to me a cluster of henna blossoms
>   from the vineyards of En Gedi. (Song 1:13-14)

> May the wine go straight to my lover,
>   flowing gently over lips and teeth. (Song 7:9)

The physical (note the way the man is working his way up his beloved's body):

> How beautiful your sandalled feet,
>   O prince's daughter!
> Your graceful legs are like jewels,
>   the work of a craftsman's hands.
> Your navel is a rounded goblet
>   that never lacks blended wine.
> Your waist is a mound of wheat
>   encircled by lilies.

> Your breasts are like two fawns,
>   twins of a gazelle.
> Your neck is like an ivory tower.
> Your eyes are the pools of Heshbon
>   by the gate of Bath Ribbam.
> Your nose is like the tower of Lebanon
>   looking towards Damascus.
> Your head crowns you like Mount Carmel.
>   Your hair is like royal tapestry;
>   the king is held captive by its tresses.
>
> How beautiful you are and how pleasing,
>   O love, with your delights! (Song 7:1-6)

Erotic anticipation:

> My lover thrust his hand through the latch-opening;
>   my heart began to pound for him. (Song 5:4)
>
> Let us go early to the vineyards
>   to see if the vines have budded,
> if their blossoms have opened,
>   and if the pomegranates are in bloom—
>   there I will give you my love. (Song 7:12)

Scripture is not obsessed with the pleasures of sex in the same way that Western society is. All the same, it is undeniably enthusiastic about sex and makes it plain to us that physical, sexual pleasure is a very good part of God's creation for a man and a woman. It is something worth celebrating, giving thanks to God.

Sex is to be companionable

The Bible talks about sex as "knowing" each other. It's a potent description, because it suggests that the whole being is engaged in sex—soul, mind and body—and that having sex reveals something of each other to each other, in a deep and lasting way. Sex should be something between spouses who are not just lovers, but companions. Even in the midst of the erotic physicality of Song of Songs, there is an emphasis on the intimate friendship of the lovers and their desire just to be with each other. Part of the erotic quest is to find one's lover, and to *keep* him or her and never have to let him or her go.

When sex is companionable, it will also be fun. When a couple is relaxed enough about sex and communicating well, sex becomes an enjoyable activity (assuming there are not other obstacles). This is not to say it isn't intense, erotic and elevating; rather, it also has at different points during sex, a more familiar, friendly and comforting aspect. Such things were part of God's antidote to loneliness for Adam. God recognized that it was *not good* for Adam to be alone, and gave to him another being from his side, a companion.

Sex is good because it draws two people together as lovers, and keeps them together as companions. There is love in the companionship, and companionship in the love. Sex achieves —ideally—both wonderful outcomes.

Chapter 2

How high is your view of sex?

We have mentioned that the Christian view of sex can be perceived as rather lofty—a kind of spiritualized ideal for a very earthy and natural human activity. The kind of sex between a married couple that we have been describing is certainly an ideal, and one worth striving for. However, it is possible to create such a romantic, unrealistic view of sex that your marriage actually buckles under its weight. Through a desire to be the best possible spouse, or through over-exposure to sex in movies, novels and magazines, a man or woman can arrive at a view of sex that actually distorts the biblical ideal by placing sex on too high a pedestal.

You can have either too lowly, or too lofty, a view of what good, godly sex is. Therefore, two simultaneous and seemingly contradictory appeals need to be made to readers:

1. Elevate your view of sex

When sex is used to sell ice cream, it's understandable that it gets devalued. Connections in the mind between sexual arousal and melting sugar do not make for a very sacred conception of sexual union. The commonality of sexual images in Western society has caused a degradation of the importance of sex, and we are encouraged to see it as but another appetite that can be easily sated. The effects of this are diverse; here are a few of them:

- virginity is something best rid of as quickly as possible
- sex is a human desire which should be fulfilled however and whenever possible
- sex need not bond two people, at least not for a lifetime
- sex and love can be separated, and sometimes need to be
- good sex is a matter of good technique and plenty of experience
- sex is an 'optional extra' in marriage, especially after a few years.

There are backlashes in some quarters, even in secular society, towards this lowly view of sex. There is commonly now an admission that sex does usually bond a man and woman, even if they don't expect it to. But the damage has been done and will take a long time to repair: sex has lost its specialness, its dignity and its exclusivity.

The pain of sexual sin—sexual abuse, failed sexual relationships, experimentation with pornography—can also cause a degradation of a person's view of sex. All of these sexual sins have powerful psychological effects upon the person who has committed them, and on those who have been victims of them. It will usually take many years for such a person to reconstruct their view of sex along biblical lines, and to work through their experience and untangle their thinking from it. (There is more on these issues in Part IV of this book.)

2. Lower your view of sex

Sex is also a very ordinary human activity engaged in by millions of people around the world everyday. It should not become the be-all and end-all of a relationship. Yes, it must be carried out in a manner pleasing to God. But God does not give out marks on orgasmic achievements; he is not interested in rating our sexual performance.

Some of the Christian husbands that Amelia sees for therapy are quite endearing in both their eagerness to bring their wives to climax, and their sense of failure for not being able to "serve her properly" in this way. The idea that one's wife must climax each time the couple has sex, or God's standards for sex are not being reached, is an over-achiever's twisting of the Scriptural command not to deprive each other but to serve each other wholeheartedly.

Furthermore, the truth that sex is about 'one-fleshness' can be exaggerated to make sex a kind of mystical experience, a physical path to spiritual expansion (or something like that!). This view of sex is promoted in the secular media and finds its way into Christian thinking, too. The one-fleshness of sexual union does not necessarily imply that each and every sexual encounter elevates the couple to heights they have never before reached. Such expectations are bound to be met with disappointment. Being one with each other does not also mean being at one with the cosmos.

Sex is messy. Sex is sweaty. It is functional and physical and amusing and clumsy and grunty. In short, it is wonderfully human, and we do ourselves a disservice by trying to make it more 'elite' than it is.

It is also possible for Christians, as much as for non-Christians, to make a fetish of sex itself and to be so focused on it that other important aspects of a marriage are neglected.

Of course, sexual problems in a marriage can be the cause of these other problems, and we are not at all saying that the sexual problems should be overlooked. We are saying that a couple can 'set the bar' of their sexual relationship so high that they in fact do damage to the relationship.

What's more, sex is simply part of God's good provision for *this life*. In the life to come, believers will no longer relate sexually. Scripture says there will be no marriage in heaven (Matt 22:29-30). This can be an upsetting thought for a couple just approaching marriage, or indeed for a couple who have been happily married for years. It is also potentially a distressing thought for someone who has lost a spouse and longs to be reunited with him or her. But the picture of the future for believers that the Bible gives us is great cause for hope and happiness. We may not have marriage, but we will have a closeness of relationship with each other that is far, far better. There will be no death, no mourning, no crying and no pain (Rev 21:4). There will be no sin to come between people (Rev 21:27). And although there will be no marriage, the image that is used to describe the way we will relate to God and Jesus Christ is as bride and husband (Rev 21:2). The happiest, most perfect aspects of marriage, will be ours to share eternally.

Since this is where we are headed, we can be realistic about the place of sex: it is a great gift for a couple in this life, but not more than that.

Chapter 3

Serving and being served

We have been talking about the 'one-fleshness' of sex, the way in which two people join in marriage in a very deep and profound way. But this does not mean that a husband ceases to be an individual, or a wife has no identity outside of being a wife. We need to explore some issues related to this, because they are important in making sure we don't misunderstand what is good and godly about sex.

Being a Christian is being other-person centred. Our Lord Jesus taught us that by example: he gave up heaven to become one of us, and to suffer for us (Phil 2). God himself is 'other-person centred', since he exists as three persons in complete union as one God. This other-person centredness has flowed into a particular way of living as a Christian. Everything we do is to be 'an act of service', as we seek to imitate our Lord, the greatest servant of them all.

This teaching is wonderful and life-changing. When you see that the universe does not revolve around you and your desires, but that you can in fact forget yourself and live for the sake of another, you become truly human. True humanity is not found in 'being an individual' but in living for others, in giving to others. That is a great Christian truth.

However, this truth can sometimes be distorted in its application to sex and intimacy. When we marry, we promise that, for better or worse, richer or poorer, we will stand by the other person, devoting ourselves to them, giving up our own desires to serve them. When two people carry out this promise, a wonderful marriage results. But this does not mean that either partner is never pleased, thrilled or excited themselves. It doesn't mean that there is no place for one's own pleasure and for focusing on yourself at certain times.

During sex, it is just as important to be able to receive pleasure freely as to give it freely. All God's good created gifts are to be received with thanksgiving (as 1 Tim 4:4 puts it), and the pleasure we feel when having sex is one of these good created things.

In fact, this is the paradox of sex: to serve your spouse, you must also focus on and enjoy your own pleasure.

If this sounds a little strange, bear with us while we explain. For a woman to enjoy sex, she needs to be aware of what her own body is telling her, to enjoy the pleasurable feelings, to give in to them and to revel in them. It is called 'erotic focus', and without it she is unlikely really to enjoy sex. She needs to be able to blank out the many thoughts racing through her mind as she approaches sex with her husband (Did I turn on that load of washing? What do the kids need for school tomorrow? Do I look fat in this underwear?) and think sexually about what they are doing. As well as loving and stroking her husband, she needs to be aware of and focus on her own body's responses to his touch, on the way he is enjoying her femininity, and on how much she wants him. As she does so, she will find herself increasingly aroused. Without being aware of her own body and freely enjoying the pleasure that it is receiving, arousal may prove elusive, and sexual union will be less than complete. One Christian sex therapist goes so far as to put it like this, "In a great marriage, mates need to build an assertive responsible selfishness. Orgasm is a great example of Christian selfishness."[1]

Likewise, a husband is to spend his life serving his wife, and this includes serving her sexually. Often it will mean delaying his own desire for climax for the sake of his wife. But this does not mean that the husband should hold back in his enjoyment during sex. He can feast on her body, relishing the way she turns him on and the intense desire he feels. He can feel his own power and energy, and really enjoy the approach of orgasm. In allowing himself to enjoy what his wife does for him sexually, he is not being selfish. He is enjoying the gift of sex as God has designed it. In fact, if he wants to please his wife, he may well find that she *requires* him to be enjoying it. During sex, she may say to him things like, "How do you feel?", "Are you enjoying this?" or "Tell me how much you like this". She is inviting him to enjoy himself, and she will be able to tell when he is—and this will increase her pleasure and arousal.

The cycle of pleasure is fascinating. Both the man and woman want to serve each other sexually. To do so, they find out what the other enjoys, and seek to provide it. But it often turns out that what the other enjoys is partly dependent on their spouse enjoying themselves. Therefore, the way of

1. Douglas E Rosenau, *A Celebration of Sex*, Thomas Nelson, Nashville, 1994, p. 52.

serving your spouse sexually has come full circle to enjoying one's own pleasure as one relates joyfully to one's spouse. The ideal scenario is two lovers enjoying their own sexual response to the sexual love that their partner is giving them.

Of course, none of this is a recommendation to actual selfishness. If a husband is only ever taking his pleasure rather than seeking his wife's pleasure, he has misunderstood the nature of intimacy. If a wife is so caught up with her arousal that her husband feels like a machine that is operating her, she needs to address this problem, because it too is wrong.

Part of sex in God's good creation is simply to enjoy the sexual response that God has given you, in the proper context of your spouse's sexual offerings. Paradoxically, this degree of 'self-focus' will lead to greater satisfaction with your relationship and greater intimacy between you.

Chapter 4

Sex in God's fallen creation

The fall of the human race into slavery to sin affected everything about us, including our sexual dimension. In fact, it is one of the most obvious areas in which sin is displayed. Although attempts have been made by various philosophers, religious leaders, rock stars and actors to separate sex from morality, human beings just don't buy it. We know that there is such a thing as sexual ethics—right and wrong sexual behaviours and attitudes. We may need some education on the details of God's instructions for sexual relations, but we all have some sense that there is right and wrong in this area.

The effects of the Fall on human intimacy are spelled out immediately in Genesis 3. Whereas in creation, the man and woman were made side-by-side, to solve the problem of the man's loneliness and to become one flesh without any sense of shame, in the Fall these experiences are all corrupted. Having sinned, the man and woman immediately feel ashamed of their nakedness. Their intimate trust and security is threatened and they seek to hide their bodies from each other. In cursing the woman for her sin, the Lord God refers both to the experience of childbirth, and to the dynamics of her relationship with her husband:

> **I will greatly increase your pains in childbearing;**
> **with pain you will give birth to children.**
> **Your desire will be for your husband,**
> **and he will rule over you. (Gen 3:16)**

The proper relations between a husband and a wife are disrupted by sin. Sin brings a change to the dynamics of the relationship, making it difficult to fulfil the plan of creation of two becoming one. Instead, there is ongoing conflict between the two parties.

The reality of sin affects every marriage. We can look at these damaging effects under several headings.

Selfishness

Although we have encouraged some degree of 'self-focus' during sex, selfishness is a very potent force for evil in a marriage. It can be expressed in little things, such as a man thoughtlessly watching the television every night instead of taking the trouble to talk with his wife, or through more major acts, such as sexual cruelty undertaken for one's own pleasure. Being selfish is being ungodly (ungodlike), because God has demonstrated over and again that he is self-sacrificial.

In biblical terms, selfishness refers to not being the kind of servant to your spouse that God would have you be: "Wives, submit to your husbands as to the Lord", writes Paul (Eph 5:22, cf. 1 Pet 3:1-2). It is selfishness for a wife not to do as Scripture says. She is acting to please herself. "Husbands, love your wives, just as Christ loved the church and gave himself up for her..." (Eph 5:25): it is selfishness for a husband not to be a self-sacrificial, Christ-like servant for his wife.

In sexual matters, selfishness means acting as if the sexual experience is not an act of unity, but one of isolated pleasure. One partner is using the other to pursue his or her own purposes. Instead of sex being something which celebrates their togetherness, it becomes a cold activity whereby each party acts according to his or her own agenda, and no meaningful interpersonal contact is made. The bodies may be adjoined, but the people have walls around them.

Sin has caused this to exist between couples. A man may treat his wife as a two-dimensional object of lust, using her body to arouse himself and satisfy his hunger, without much thought as to her experience of the act. A woman may not respond to her husband's needs, nor give him any warmth or encouragement or welcome. Instead, she may resolutely pursue her own agenda during sex, whether it be making it as quick as possible, exploring some mental fantasy which doesn't involve her husband, or not focusing at all on what they are doing but blocking out the sexual activity altogether. These common female reactions to sex are all sins of selfishness.

Unfaithfulness

From the creation account itself, we see that God meant sex to be an activity exclusive to two people united in marriage, leaving their parents to forge an independent family (Gen 2:24). The marriage commitment is one of faithfulness and exclusivity in the face of all other temptations and opportunities. It is a covenant (or 'binding agreement') as Malachi 2:14 puts it. God's relationship to his people, Israel, is itself described in terms of a marriage where God is always faithful, while Israel wavers. Israel fails to keep its exclusive covenant commitment to God. This theological model for faithfulness is important, because it helps us understand just how much God is aggrieved by unfaithfulness at any level.

All sexual sin committed within marriage is an expression of unfaithfulness towards one's spouse. It can be a calculated unfaithfulness, as in an extended affair, or a spontaneous unfaithfulness, as in a foolish one-night stand—it makes no difference how it occurs, it is all unfaithfulness to the covenant you have made with one another. Unfaithfulness need not always go so far as physical, sexual expression either. As Jesus taught, the adulterous intention of our hearts is just as much an expression of adultery as the act itself (Matt 5:27-8). Our 'thought lives' are a battleground for faithfulness, and one which we must not ignore or let lapse. "Put to death, therefore, whatever belongs to your earthly nature: sexual immorality, impurity, lust, evil desires and greed, which is idolatry", Colossians 3:5 teaches. "Because of these, the wrath of God is coming."

Of course, faithfulness to one's spouse is not only a matter of controlling your sexual urges and actions. Faithfulness means being true to your promises to love and care for each other for better for worse, for richer for poorer, in sickness and in health. When we break these promises by neglecting our spouse, and failing to love and cherish him or her, we are being unfaithful. In our modern context this can be expressed in all sorts of ways: over-commitment to work, the intrusion of other close friendships, always putting children before your spouse, pursuing a career at the expense of your relationship, and so forth. Faithfulness in marriage requires hard-headed decision-making which places the marriage first above all other worldly priorities. The apostle Paul does not mince words about how difficult faithfulness can be: "Because of the present crisis, I think that it is good for you to remain as you are… [t]hose who marry will face many troubles in this life, and I want to spare you this" (1 Cor 7:26, 28).

The apostle's words testify to the conflict between sex and marriage in creation, and sex and marriage in the fallen world. In the former, marriage is an ideal state, a celebrated state, a wondrous union with no sense of shame or failure. This is the view of marriage we often have as we set out on it. But in the fallen state, marriage does not live up to this ideal. It retains some elements of its glory, some aspects of that marvellous union of beings, but it suffers greatly under the reign of sin.

Great is your faithfulness

Faithfulness is the biggest challenge for a husband. Sexual faithfulness means delighting in your wife to the exclusion of all other women. It doesn't mean rejecting other women *holus bolus*, pretending that you hate them, but it does mean creating an exclusive pleasure in your own wife.

Solomon said, "A faithful man will be richly blessed" (Proverbs 28:20). But he also said, eight chapters earlier, "A faithful man who can find?" (20:6).

This is the great challenge to today's Christian men. Can we, in the midst of pornographic advertising, workplace temptations to immorality, strains upon our relationships with our wives, create in our minds, hearts and loins, an exclusive sexual fanaticism for our wives? Those who do will be richly rewarded.

Story

Grant and Christine had been married for three years when it was discovered that Grant had been surreptitiously downloading pornographic images at his workplace for many months. He was horrified when his supervisor found him out and he lost his job. He couldn't believe how stupid he had been, but he just hadn't been able to resist the easy access to sexual images. It had become a lunchtime addiction.

When he told his wife, she too was devastated. It made her feel worthless, unattractive and angry. It was like she meant nothing to her husband. He protested that he loved only her, that this was simply lust, that he was thoroughly ashamed, and that it would not happen again. She found this impossible to believe.

Two big problems have emerged for the couple. First, the wife has had to deal with the blow to her self-esteem. Can she trust her husband when he says he loves her, but is unfaithful in this way? Can she deal with the self-doubt that the incident raised: why did he want to look at those women? Second, the husband has to protect himself against his addictive tendency to ensure it doesn't happen in the future. He needs to put in place structures which make it less likely that he will be tempted by pornographic images. He also has to re-earn the trust of his wife, by displaying over and over again his commitment to her.

The fact that they have talked about the issue, and that they sought the help of outsiders, suggests that they have a better than average chance of improving their relationship over time. But it's going to be tough, and a long haul. Once trust has been broken, it is hard indeed to re-earn it.

Untamed bodies

The most obvious threat to sexual happiness and contentment in the fallen world comes from our lack of control over our bodies. Romans 1:18-32 presents an infamous catalogue of sins—many sexual—which those who reject God pursue as if enslaved to them. The work of the spirit of Christ in the heart of believers releases people from this slavery to sin, but the effects of sin on our sexual make-up are still present. Later in Romans, Paul writes: "For in my inner being I delight in God's law; but I see another law at work in the members of my body, waging war against the law of my mind and making me a prisoner of the law of sin at work within my members" (Rom 7:22-23). In the sinful world, even for the Christian believer, passions get distorted, desires messed up, and sin wages war on our bodies.

God's will for Christian people in this fallen world is that we learn to control our bodies and not give ourselves over to their lusts and evil inclinations. He has called us to live holy lives and reject impurity (1 Thess 4:3-8). We are to "flee" from sexual immorality (1 Cor 6:18). One of the aids God gives us to help us flee is marriage, and although it doesn't sound very romantic, in places the Bible describes marriage as a safeguard against immorality (1 Cor 7:2, 9; 1 Tim 5:14). This is not to say that marriage is by any means a guarantee against sexual sin: married people still live under the same curse of sin as do the unmarried. Rather, marriage provides a strong and obvious structure within which a couple can work at controlling their bodies and their desires.

Honesty

Honesty about whom you find attractive may diffuse the dishonest secret of a one-sided attraction. Some couples find that, even though it might hurt a little at first to admit to each other that they find someone else attractive, the very admission quickly decreases the significance of the event and enables you to laugh and move on.

Talk about whether this approach would work for you.

The time is short

The teaching of the apostle Paul in 1 Corinthians 7 makes fascinating reading for those who have decided to marry. Paul makes the following points:

- it is good for a man or woman not to marry (vv. 8, 37-38)
- it is preferable for a widow not to remarry (v. 40)
- neither husbands nor wives should deprive each other sexually (v. 5)
- marrying is preferable to immorality (v. 9)
- married men and women are distracted from the service of God (vv. 32-35)
- married people should not be engrossed in marriage (vv. 29-31)

At first reading, this passage seems to degrade marriage terribly. It makes it at best a means of avoiding sexual immorality and at worst something which prevents you from devoting yourself to the Lord in body and spirit (v. 34). However, on reflection it is a very important and encouraging passage for those entering marriage.

Paul teaches that "the time is short" and "this world in its present form is passing away" (1 Cor 7:29, 31). Nothing in this age is permanent; nothing is perfect; everything is waiting on the judgment of God and the renewal of all things, as promised in the gospel of Jesus. Christians are waiting for God to fulfil his plan of salvation and to make plain to all that Jesus is Lord of heaven and earth. Getting married needs to be understood as simply part of what we are doing while we are waiting.

This may sound unromantic, but it actually gives a very dignified and wonderful role to marriage: it is a means by which God's people wait on him in a manner worthy of him. By marrying, we seek to serve another person in a Christlike fashion (for the husband), or submit to another person in the manner of the church's submission to Christ (for the wife). We aim to be sexually pure by totally devoting our sexual attentions to this one person. And we hope to raise a family whom we will teach to love and fear God and his commandments. Whilst the Bible says it is better not to marry, it also says that the person who marries does the right thing. For many people (perhaps for most), marriage is the best way of living a life that is pleasing to God while waiting for "the glorious appearing of our great God and Saviour, Jesus Christ" (Titus 2:13).

Story

Daniel is a delightful 22-year-old man. He is currently considering asking his slightly older girlfriend to marry him. She has confided in him that she slept with her previous boyfriend, despite both of them being Christians. Daniel is devastated. He is torn between not entering the relationship—he had always hoped to marry a virgin—but also hating himself for being like this and thinking that he should be able to forgive.

Daniel is mourning a loss of expectation. The world is

fallen, and sexual sin has caused and continues to cause great suffering, not only to those who were involved in it but to others, too. In one sense, Daniel's is a right reaction. It's not just OK that your partner has slept with someone. However, he wants to offer forgiveness, and knows that he himself will bring disappointment to his girlfriend in many ways if they stay together. He is currently trying to come to terms with what it will mean to accept that sin has damaged his future marriage partner in this way, while at the same time reflecting on his own sinfulness and his need for forgiveness from God (and potentially from his future partner) in other areas.

 Discuss together the expectations you had as a teenager about your future marriage partner? Did you expect to marry someone who was sexually pure? Did you expect to be sexually pure yourself? How might your expectations affect the marriage into which you are now heading?

Is the situation hopeless?

This discussion may seem a little depressing for a book about the delights of sex. Surely we could have cut to the chase. But we are trying to communicate the seriousness of sin, and the fact that both you and your spouse are caught up in sin's entanglements. Fortunately, as Christians, you have a way forward and can protect your marriage against the assaults of sexual sin.

To cope with sex in the fallen world, we are given the following guidelines in the New Testament:

1. 1 Corinthians 7:8-9: If your sexual desires are strong, and you are finding that you cannot control yourself, Paul's advice is to get married. Don't be a fool and burn with passion; do something about it. No doubt many of us will take this path, but this is a matter for prayer. If you are not already married or engaged, can you respond to God's word in 1 Corinthians 7 by praying that God would relieve you of the "many troubles" of marriage in this life?

2. 1 Corinthians 7:3-5: Husbands and wives shouldn't deny each other sex. This sounds negative and dutiful. It's not; it's positive and dutiful. It says sex can take priority over other aspects of marriage—and we shouldn't refuse it for lesser things. Instead, make sure you devote yourself to serving your spouse in this way. Husbands, don't deny wives; wives, don't deny husbands. Engaged couples may be thinking that this is almost laughably unlikely, but beware: you may think differently the other side of the wedding night.

3. Hebrews 13:4: "Marriage should be honoured by all, and the marriage bed kept pure, for God will judge the adulterer and all the sexually immoral". The marriage relationship is sacred. Cling to your spouse, and don't let anyone get between you (literally or figuratively). Devote your sexual energies to your spouse, to the exclusion of all other lovers, real or imagined. There is a fabulous section in Proverbs which makes this point very poetically and memorably. It is the kind of passage that a husband does well to learn and remember:

> **Drink water from your own cistern,**
> > **running water from your own well.**
> **Should your springs overflow into the streets,**
> > **your streams of water in the public squares?**
> **Let them be yours alone,**

> never to be shared with strangers.
> May your fountain be blessed,
>   and may you rejoice in the wife of your youth.
> A loving doe, a graceful deer—
>   may her breasts satisfy you, always,
>   may you ever be captivated by her love.
> Why be captivated, my son, by an adulteress?
>   Why embrace the bosom of another man's wife?
>
> (Prov 5:15-20)

4. Utilize the resource of sexual differences that God has given to men and women. We will explore this resource throughout the rest of the book. It was because it was "not good for the man to be alone" that God created the woman. The man needed something that the woman could offer. Their complementary natures provide many of the resources required to ensure a good, godly sex life and a long, fruitful marriage.

Part II

The basics

Chapter 5

Actually, what is sex?

The former President of the United States of America, Bill Clinton, became embroiled in a fascinating, if prurient public debate: is oral sex actually sex? Legally, the President fought on, but on the streets most people knew that he had been engaged in sex with Monica Lewinsky. The definition of sex was widely accepted to include the kinds of activities that took place between these two people.

As disturbing and circus-like as the Clinton-Lewinsky matter was, it did bring to the fore the notion that sex is not restricted to genital intercourse. Sex involves far more than that. But, as many people find out first hand, the human temptation is always to push the boundaries of what is defined as sex and what is not—the boundaries always being moved to expand the range of what fits a legalistic definition.

Drawing the line

Where on this line do you think a Christian couple should stop when they are going out or engaged? How do you justify your position? Which activities would you call 'sex'?

Holding hands	hugging	kissing	sexual touching outside clothes	sexual touching inside clothes	heavy petting	mutual masturbation to orgasm	oral sex	intercourse

∝⌒⊚

Sex is more than intercourse. It is also 'outercourse'. This fabulous word refers to all the activity that causes sexual arousal but doesn't involve the joining of the genitals. In the Scriptures, and in many contemporary definitions of sexual behaviour, it is all sex. Intercourse is definitely sex. Outercourse is also sex. Sex is anything that results in the sexual arousal of one or both of the people involved.

Sex is physical behaviour between people which bonds them physically and emotionally. A certain kind of hugging can be sexual, as can a certain kind of kissing, or even a certain kind of hand-holding! Perhaps you are laughing as you read this and imagining an uptight Christian couple who never hold hands until the wedding day. Before you are too judgemental, let the idea ring for a while. Think about it: do you know a way of holding your boyfriend or fiance or husband's hand that can arouse him sexually? Yes? That is what we mean.

Christianity is always interested in our hearts, and we know in our hearts when we are involved in sexual behaviour. We know that we are becoming aroused; we can see the reaction of arousal in our partner's eyes. We have to be honest with ourselves and each other. And if a girl is naïve about the effect that she is having by stroking her boyfriend's hand during the Sunday night sermon, then he had better tell her about it and see if she can be loving enough to stop.

There is a mountain of discussion that could take place over these matters, and we'll leave these for another book. In this book for married or marrying couples, we are talking more about the doing than the abstaining.

Outercourse in marriage

It is a bizarre fact that many of those exciting activities which Christians are trying desperately to avoid during courtship and engagement, are in fact the very things that are important in maintaining a good sexual relationship during marriage. We tend to do them when we're not supposed to, and STOP doing them when they would be great! Men tend to be motivated to do these things when going out, but not so much when married (that is, they are happy to woo their partners before marriage, but not when she is a "sure thing"). Women seem sometimes to be happy to be involved in 'sex play' during courtship, for the benefits of intimacy that they bring, but then miss out on 'godly seduction' once married because their husbands race straight towards intercourse now that they can.

Men: women enjoy outercourse. In fact, many women report that their most exciting and satisfying sexual experiences are outercourse, usually as a guilty pleasure of courtship. There is a problem here that husbands need to address, and that wives need to make their husbands aware of. If we believe that all of these kinds of activities are sex, then we should include them in our sex life as a married couple.

Outercourse

If we believe that all of these activities are part of sex, then why do they so often cease when a couple gets married? This may seem inconceivable to those readers who are just about to embark on marriage—you are probably champing at the bit and looking forward to enjoying all and every one of these activities. However, it is commonly reported (especially by women, but also by men) that activities such as:

hand-holding
neck-rubbing
hair-stroking
non-sexual cuddling
passionate kissing
looking fondly into each other's eyes
saying 'I love you' over and over
smiling invitingly
and just holding each other for a long, long time…

…fade away very quickly once the ring is placed on the finger. Try re-introducing them to your marriage!

Chapter 6

The four stages of sexual arousal

en and women go through four stages of arousal. Each stage is part of the sexual act, and needs to be understood if sex is to be satisfying for a couple. It is valuable to see each phase as important, or sex gets reduced to just intercourse and orgasm. It is also important to understand the different responses and interests that men and women have in the four stages.

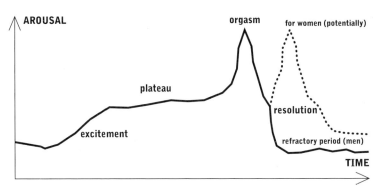

Excitement

The excitement phase begins with mental and/or physical stimulation—for some people, one word is enough to get it started. Others are stimulated less readily. The man will quickly get an erect penis while, less noticeably, the woman's vagina will lubricate and engorge. For both men and women, their heart rates and blood pressure will increase, and many will get a sexual flush. The man's arousal is a combination of sensory input (looking at his wife, sexual touching, the scents of sex) and physical attention to erogenous zones, which can be found all over the body. The woman's arousal is similarly a combination of good thoughts and feelings with physical attention, but it is less predictable than that of the male. A woman's sexual excitement may begin with her husband chatting tenderly to her as he unpacks the dishwasher. It may take her longer to 'warm up' to sexual touching, but once there, she too will become excited by physical attention to her erogenous zones. As a general rule, women tend to like their peripheries touched first and their genitals last, and for this journey to take some minutes. A wife needs to tell her husband where and how she likes to be touched, as this can be extremely specific to the individual. For example, she may or may not like her clitoris to be touched directly. There is no way for a husband to know this unless he is told.

For the male, the excitement stage has a rapid onset and a short duration, but it can be rekindled just as quickly if something interrupts the sexual experience (such as a crying baby). For the female, the excitement stage has a slower onset but can continue for quite some time (such as for hours over an extended romantic dinner).

Plateau

If the initial excitement is pursued, the couple will move on to the plateau phase. Here the sex organs of both men and women continue to become flushed and engorged as they prepare themselves for intercourse. This is usually the longest and most enjoyable phase of sex, especially for the woman. It is common at this stage for the man to have some emission of fluid from the penis; this is normal, and is known as 'pre-ejaculate'. It contains sperm so can, of course, impregnate a woman if intercourse is taking place. It is important to know this, since it affects your approach to birth control (see details of birth control options below).

This very pleasurable stage of sex allows the couple to enjoy each other in increasingly intense loveplay. It is the stage for experimenting with different kinds of touch, different sexual positions, and periods of intercourse. It should be enjoyed at leisure!

Orgasm

Although the orgasm is the shortest phase in the sexual cycle, it is the one that often receives the most attention, being given an almost mythical status as the ultimate quest of human relations. An orgasm is, by definition, a moment of sexual peak, but it is also just a part of the sexual relationship and shouldn't be thought of as the ultimate goal. Orgasms are most enjoyable when they are part of a sexual cycle that is enjoyable as a whole.

The physical experience of orgasm is intense. In both men and women, there is a strong contraction of muscles in the penis and vagina, respectively. There is also involuntary muscular spasm in the pelvis and across the body. The man experiences ejaculation, in a series of short bursts. The breathing and heart rates of the couple are elevated. There is a myth that men always experience ejaculation as a volcanic explosion, but the truth is that there is variety in the male experience, as there is in the female experience. Orgasms and ejaculations can be extraordinarily intense, or they can be milder and more diffuse. Women often experience orgasm as "waves of pleasure" or a "flooding feeling"; men often report a sense of "explosion", "like a train approaching" or "a tremendous release of pressure". In short, there is a range of normal orgasmic experience.

One difference stands out between men and women. Men have a recovery (or refractory) period following ejaculation, where they are not capable of another orgasm. In young men, this period can be a matter of a few minutes; as men age, the refractory period usually increases to a few hours or even days. However, women do not have this refractory period. They are capable of having repeated orgasms within minutes of each other, or in rapid succession. Once you know this, it can become an unnecessary pressure upon a couple. The husband may think that he hasn't performed adequately if he can't bring his wife to multiple orgasms; the wife may feel unsexy if she doesn't experience them. This is ridiculous, and returns our attention to the problem of making the orgasm the holy grail of sex. The point is not to be a 'sexual legend'; the point is that you enjoy sex as a whole, together, in whatever way brings you both pleasure. If this involves multiple orgasms, bully for you.

Another revered sexual goal is the simultaneous orgasm, where husband and wife experience orgasm at the same time (one sexual theorist even suggests that it ought to be with the couple looking into each other's eyes). We feel that this, too, makes sex an Olympic event and raises the bar of sexual happiness way beyond what is necessary. Some couples may enjoy simultaneous orgasms; some may enjoy orgasms a few minutes apart; some may find that there needs to be a time differential between their climaxes in order that they both enjoy the experience. The goal is to find what kinds of sexual patterns suit you as a couple, not to achieve any externally set goals of what should constitute good sex.

Resolution

After orgasm, both men and women have a release of tension and their bodies relax until they return to the unaroused state. Blood leaves the genitals; muscles relax; skin flush disappears slowly. The heart rate and breathing return to normal, or even lower than normal rates. Some people's genitals become very sensitive during this phase, and it can be uncomfortable to touch them. Again, you will need to talk as a couple about what you like.

It is classically reported that men and women want to do different things in this stage. Women want to bask in the afterglow of sexual pleasure—cuddle each other, stroke each other's hair and skin, talk quietly and intimately, look into each other's eyes. This prolongs the sexual experience for the woman and makes her feel loved and desired. It fulfils the companionship aspect of sex. Men, by and large, want to go to sleep. His sexual release overwhelms him with tiredness, and he finds it hard to summon the energy to do almost anything. This is potentially an area of conflict for the couple, and one where you will need to serve each other. A man might decide to sit up in bed so that he doesn't immediately succumb to tiredness, and cuddle his wife for a few minutes. A wife might decide that she will let her husband sleep, and stroke his hair while he does so, after he has told her he loves her. Communication about needs and desires is, once more, the key to happiness in the resolution phase.

Part III

Starting out

Chapter 7

Sex before marriage

reparing for sex is only one aspect of preparing for marriage, but it is linked closely to lots of other matters. We will try to deal with these as best we can in a short space, but we recommend that you supplement this book with some further thinking on other areas of married life: communication (in particular), financial planning (a much bigger stressor in marriage than most people imagine before they get married), and the biblical teaching on the relationship between a husband and wife. The reading list at the end of this book provides some suggested titles.

The truth of the matter is that many Christian people arrive at the point of marriage having already had some sexual experiences. This is terribly sad, and an outcome of living in this fallen creation. We have all sinned, and many of us have sinned sexually. We can rationalize it all we like ("I was young", "It was my brother's fault for showing me the magazines", "It was natural sexual exploration", "If I'd known that I was going to marry you, I wouldn't have done it"), but we must name it as sin.

It is best to face this reality, and to deal with its effects upon your marriage—even if it is sexual experience prior to marriage between you and your spouse-to-be.

Sexual activity before marriage may have taken any of the following forms:

- sexual experimentation as a child with other children
- sexual abuse of a child by an adult
- sexual contact with your spouse-to-be: foreplay and/or intercourse
- sexual contact with people other than your spouse-to-be: foreplay and/or intercourse
- homosexual experiences
- masturbation
- sexual fantasy, including pornography.

All of these events will have an impact on how you and your spouse will relate sexually. Your 'sexual profile' as a couple will be unique, but there will be elements of your experience that will be common to many people. Some of these experiences will have a greater impact than others, although it is dangerous to underestimate the importance of even short-lived or seemingly minor sexual encounters. Sex affects us at a deep level, and its impact is felt for many years to come.

How should a couple who is preparing for marriage, or a married couple who has not yet dealt with previous sexual experience, go about facing this reality? Here are our suggestions:

1. *Decide together how you are going to talk about your past experiences.* In our view, it is better to talk in quite some detail about past sexual experiences before getting married. This idea generates great anxiety in people, and fear that they will

be rejected. However, this anxiety and fear is best dealt with at this stage rather than down the track in married life when the consequences may be more serious. If you are going to be married, your spouse has the right to know about these experiences, since they affect him or her. You need to talk lovingly, generously, openly and patiently. But you can also express your emotions in relation to what your future spouse is telling you: we must be honest with each other. If you are angry, be angry. If you are devastated, say so. Only by truly communicating these responses can you hope to move on together. You may need to ask questions of each other, such as "Have you had experiences with pornography?" or "Is there anything important sexually about your past that you are finding it hard to tell me?" These are very painful questions, and the answers may emerge slowly and awkwardly, but talking about these things will in most cases build greater trust between you and be beneficial to your marriage.

This may all take quite some time and many conversations. It can be horrible to imagine going through the process, but it is one of the costs of your previous experiences—even if you were not responsible for them, such as in the case of sexual abuse.

2. *Recognize that your first sexual experiences are likely to have had a major impact on how you think and feel about sex.* They tend to become memories imprinted on the body and mind, often played over and extended or distorted during the years that follow. You will need to be honest with yourself about this, and then share honestly with your spouse.

3. *Pray and recognize that God is willing to forgive sexual sin (both yours and that of others) and wants you to pursue holy living from now on.* You may still find it difficult to deal with

your thoughts and feelings about sex, even when you know you are forgiven. No-one is suggesting it is simply a matter of "forgive and forget"—if only it could be that straightforward. It may still be psychologically very difficult to accept God's forgiveness or to forgive others, and may cause ongoing sexual issues for the people affected (see Part IV for further information).

If there are ongoing problems here, it may be useful to seek the help of a pastor or counsellor.

Chapter 8

Having a good honeymoon

What is your image of the honeymoon? An idyllic time of uninterrupted pleasure? A sexual paradise in which you both finally enjoy what you have been wanting for so long? The best holiday you are ever likely to have? Is it anything like the following?

Story

Jeff and Edina had a great courtship, full of fun and trying hard not to end up in bed together. They were very eager for the honeymoon to begin. When they tried to have intercourse on the wedding night, they found it impossible. They were both keen and relaxed—anxiety was not an issue—but Edina had an imperforate hymen. The entrance to her vagina was almost completely covered over by the hymenal skin. They were unable to have sex until they had returned from their honeymoon and had the skin snipped by a doctor. Their sex life was not affected, due to their buoyant sense of humour, but for more anxious couples it could have been an utter disaster.

Honeymoons are unpredictable. They can be great; they can be nightmares. And the more stories we hear, the higher grows the percentage of nightmares! But it need not be that way, if you start thinking about it now.

If you are not yet married, now is the time to talk about your expectations for the honeymoon. How often are you expecting to have sex on the honeymoon? Are you planning to have sex on the wedding night? Have you even considered the possibility that you might not have penetrative intercourse on the wedding night itself? Are you going to do everything together every day, or are you going to have some time alone? There are plenty of questions to talk about.

There's a feeling that if you don't enjoy your honeymoon, there must be something seriously amiss in your relationship. It is as if the honeymoon has to be the best moment of the marriage to come, the high point which you will always look back on.

But the reality is that a lot of people find their honeymoon very difficult, for a whole host of reasons. This is not surprising, given what is taking place. Let's step back and consider what is going on as you lead up to your honeymoon:

- you are about to make a lifelong commitment to one person
- you have been planning a wedding day, which usually involves months of decision-making, spending and detailed planning
- you are expecting this day to be one of, if not the, best day of your life
- you are bringing together at least two family networks that may or may not get along with each other
- you are embarking on a sexual relationship
- you are probably moving into a new and unfamiliar house, if not both of you, at least one of you.

This combination of factors makes the whole wedding event a very significant stressor for both parties. Stress and relaxing holidays with lots of sexual pleasure don't go together!

The good news is that you can plan practically for your honeymoon. It requires a bit of foreknowledge, a bit of putting aside what you dream or hope will happen and 'suspending disbelief' that it might not be the magical mystery tour you have always imagined. If you can leave aside this dream for a moment, and imagine some of the real and practical issues involved, then you should actually have a great time. Who knows, it might even approximate your wildest dreams.

Following are some important considerations for everyone who is approaching marriage and hoping for a great honeymoon.

1. Birth control

Do go to your local doctor before you get married and discuss what is involved in entering a sexual relationship. If you can do this together, all the better. This book spells out some basic information below, but there are also books which describe sexual functioning to a degree which we don't here. See the reading list at the end of the book for suggestions.

One of the significant issues to discuss is birth control.

Birth control needs to be discussed well before the wedding night, and a mutually satisfactory arrangement reached. You may find, as a Christian couple, that this raises issues where you differ, and it is good to sort these things through before marriage. For instance, the woman may not be happy with taking the contraceptive pill, but the man has always expected this and does not want to use condoms. This needs to be discussed, and a solution found, if you are going to begin your sexual relationship happily.

Contraception is increasingly a minefield for people who have ethical priorities. We have to cope with the blessing and curse of choice. This means we need to take responsibility for our actions and their consequences in this area. There are some plainly unacceptable methods of birth control for Christians; there are some which are arguably OK; there are others which seem to pose no problems. Furthermore, this is an area in which change is rapid. We can only briefly outline the options currently available, but suggest that you do some research into the birth control you choose to use to ensure that you understand how it affects your body and how it prevents conception and pregnancy.

The unacceptable

The basic Christian idea is that life begins at conception, that is, when the ovum (egg) and sperm meet. So, any birth control device which allows conception, but then prevents further development of the embryo must be avoided. This includes intra-uterine devices (IUDs) and the morning-after pill.

You may find that non-Christian doctors find it difficult to 'tune in' to your priorities and ethical concerns in this area. Doctors may mention some unacceptable contraceptive methods in a matter-of-fact way, as if all methods are alike. This is not the case; Christians need to understand the way such medications and procedures operate in order that they don't end up doing something they will regret. Ask your doctor for specific information about the various methods.

The acceptable

We have listed the acceptable methods of contraception, in order of effectiveness, from least effective to most effective. However, there are still some aspects of some of these methods which raise serious and important ethical questions beyond the scope of this book. We have tried to provide the information you require to begin thinking about whether or not to use these methods.

i. Withdrawal

This involves removing the penis from the vagina before ejaculation. It is not a very effective method of preventing pregnancy, for two basic reasons. First, it is difficult to practise; and second, sperm may leave the penis before ejaculation (the pre-ejaculate). It is not a particularly satisfying way to have sex either, since all the effort on the man's part is dedicated to *not* going where he wants to go! Having said all that, it is still relatively common and may be a suitable approach at different stages of married life (for instance, if other contraceptive methods are not available and you don't mind becoming pregnant!).

ii. The Sympto-Thermal Method (STM)

This is a combination of methods known as the rhythm method, Billings method, calendar method, ovulation method, cervical mucus and temperature methods. If both partners are entirely committed to it, it can be effective. It is often practised by those opposed to all contraception. There are books which go into the details of how to do this,[1] but here's a basic outline.

1. There is also an organization which teaches people how to use this method. There are kits available from chemists. You can also contact the Australian Council of Natural Family Planning: www.acnfp.com.au. Similar national bodies exist in other countries—try the internet.

It relies on the natural cycle of the woman. The most fertile period of the month is the middle of the cycle (two weeks before the next period). This is the time when the ovum is released from the ovary into the fallopian tube. This can sometimes be mildly painful for the woman, and sex itself can be uncomfortable at this time. However, it is the time when conception is most likely, because the egg is in the optimum place for the sperm to meet it. This is the time to avoid sexual intercourse if conception is not desirable.

Other ways of identifying this fertile period is that the cervical mucus becomes more watery and clear. A problem that emerges is that because of hormonal activity, a woman often feels most like having sex at this time!

This is a good contraceptive option if you are very motivated, and if pregnancy is not entirely unwelcome.

iii. Condoms

Thanks to the 'Safe Sex' campaigns of the 1980s, a lot of people use this method. It has been promoted since the escalation of AIDS because of its benefits in avoiding venereal disease. It also has the advantage of allowing the man to take responsibility for contraception. It is quite straightforward: the erect penis is sheathed with a tube of latex before penetration, so that the sperm is caught in the tip. The condom is removed after the penis has been withdrawn.

There are potential problems with this method, and it is not foolproof. The condom must be used properly. It requires some practice to put on successfully, so if it is being put on in the dark in a hurry, the possibility of not doing it properly is increased. Sperm can escape around the side of the condom, and condoms do break. The man might practise putting it on before the wedding night.

Furthermore, both men and women report some discomfort using condoms. Some women find vaginal dryness and lack of lubrication mean that the penis does not feel comfortable in the vagina when it is sheathed. Many men also report loss of sensation and lowering of pleasure when using condoms. Such things can lead to lower compliance with the contraceptive method.

There is now a female condom available which transmits body warmth (it is made of PVC). It makes a rustling noise (!) but is gaining acceptance and some women find it quite comfortable.

iv. The oral contraceptive Pill

This is a very valuable method of birth control, and one used by many women. It is sometimes a little maligned because of the way it leaves responsibility for contraception with the woman. However there is no reason that a husband shouldn't be involved, through understanding what the Pill does and helping his wife to remember to take it.

There are two significantly different versions of the Pill. The first is the 'combined Pill', which contains oestregen and progesterone. This puts the woman's body into a false state of pregnancy where she doesn't ovulate: there is no egg to be fertilized. It is quite safe and convenient. There are some potential side-effects: breast tenderness, slight weight gain and sometimes depression. If ovulation does in fact occur (for instance, if you forget to take it), the combined Pill will not affect the developing baby and implantation in the uterus will occur normally.

The second version of the Pill is the 'progesterone-only' Pill, also known as the 'mini-Pill'. It is often prescribed for breastfeeding women, who cannot take the combined Pill because it affects milk supply. There are some potential ethical dilemmas surrounding it. Its primary mode of action is to thicken the cervical mucus, making it inhospitable to sperm. It doesn't necessarily affect ovulation in the usual course. However, it does affect the lining of the uterus to the extent that *sometimes* implantation of an embryo is impossible. This means that, in the unlikely event of ovulation and fertilization, an embryo will be unable to implant. The progesterone-only Pill needs to be taken at the same time every day to work effectively and it has its range of side effects as well.

v. Implants

These are a relatively new form of contraception with increasing popularity. They are tiny rods that are slipped beneath the skin after a minor incision by a doctor. They slowly release a low dose of progesterone to thicken the cervical mucus and often lead to suppression of ovulation, too. They can remain in the body for a number of years but can be removed very easily. Normal fertility appears to be readily restored. However, it is stressed that this is quite a new form of contraception, so long-term studies are not yet available.

vi. Injections

This involves a doctor injecting progesterone into a muscle once every three months. It has been practised for much longer than implants and is very effective. More women seem to acclimatize to this form of contraception than to the implants, but injections can have a greater impact on the woman's cycle and can affect later fertility. It takes some time for the effect of the injections to wear off after ceasing use.

vii. Diaphragms/cervical caps

A diaphragm is a small latex device that covers the cervix and prevents sperm entering. A doctor fits the device at first (however, they are somewhat out of vogue with doctors). It is then inserted by the woman before sex and removed 12 hours afterwards. Many women prefer this method and don't find it difficult since they are used to using tampons during their periods. Usually, women cannot feel the diaphragm when it has been inserted. It is also popular because it is an alternative to taking hormone-altering medications such as the Pill.

Sometimes, women become more comfortable with using diaphrams after they have been sexually active for a while. It is a very safe and acceptable method.

viii. Vasectomy and tubal ligation

This is the ultimate form of contraception, but it must be considered irreversible. It is a surgical procedure. It must be undertaken with the full understanding that there will be no pregnancies from this point onwards—successful reversal is highly unlikely.

Again, we emphasize the value of visiting a doctor as a couple and talking through contraceptive options well before the wedding.

2. Not too much, not too little

People choose lots of different kinds of honeymoons. Some travel miles; some stay home. Some want adventure; some can think of nothing worse. You need to tailor your honeymoon to the things you both find relaxing. If you are not bushwalkers, don't make this your opportunity to start. If you hate lying around doing nothing on beaches, perhaps you need to make sure the honeymoon isn't *too* low-key.

We feel that it is best to do neither too much nor too little.

It's a big holiday, this one. It is most likely your first extended time together alone. It's a chance to turn off from the stress of the wedding itself, a chance to pause before you launch into the next phase of life. It is a very special time, but it is also a very unusual time and not in-and-of-itself immediately relaxing. An enormous change will have just occurred. You are revolutionizing your life in becoming a couple. You need to take all of this into account when planning the kind of holiday you need.

You do need time to unwind and actually feel like you can just relax together. However, you also need to recall that you are having a holiday in order to return to a new life together, not putting it off for as long as possible! We have known couples who have holidayed on as long as possible and found it very hard to return to a 'normal' life together. We have known many more couples who feel like they never had that early holiday they needed, either because they didn't have the money, or the time, or didn't think it mattered that much.

3. Honeymoon expectations

As we have said, the key to a happy honeymoon is to talk about both of your expectations beforehand. But you do also need to be flexible. You can't predict how you will both react to the wedding itself, and to the realization that you have 'tied the knot'. Be realistic about the level of stress involved in getting married. On psychological scales which measure stress, marriage compares with the death of a family member!

Honeymoon planning

Do this exercise as a couple. Answer the questions separately at first, and then discuss your answers. What differences are there? How can you deal with these different expectations?

How much sex?

How much sleeping?

How active will we be?

When will we spend time together?

When will we spend time alone?

What else do we want to achieve?

One of the biggest issues of the honeymoon will be your sexual expectations. Of course, couples really look forward to the wedding night, and the days and weeks that will follow. But experiences of this period will differ widely. Think back to the scenarios which began this book. Did any of them shock you? Did you relate to any of them (or think that they might be you)? Find time to chat together about your hopes and fears for the wedding night.

Sex is an art and a skill. It requires practice, talent, playing to your strengths and working on your weaknesses. People get anxious about their performance on the honeymoon, especially if one partner has more sexual experience than the other. The reality is that *you are very unlikely to have your best sex on your honeymoon*. Unless you have already been in a sexual relationship with your new spouse for a long time before you get married, you will not know each other well enough to have your 'best sex'. Even if you do know each other this way, the fact of the wedding may throw a spanner in the works.

It is best to think of the wedding night and the honeymoon as the *beginning* of something great, rather than the goal that has been reached. It is a wonderful starting point for developing your sexual relationship. This suggestion leads to the advice below.

4. Take it slowly

Amelia often encourages couples who have been very physically circumspect while going out not to feel that they need immediately to have intercourse on the wedding night. As we have said, sex involves a whole range of intimate, exclusive acts by which you express your 'one-fleshness'. Intercourse is the goal, but there is nothing wrong with taking some time to reach the goal. It can be good to move towards intercourse, rather than immediately jump to it. Women, in particular, warm up slowly; so does your sexual relationship together.

Lots of couples who have been too intimate while engaged think that there is no way they will have trouble on the honeymoon. They are just so eager to have sex, they can't imagine anything getting in the way. But there are plenty of things that can. They too should take things a little slower than expected. They can become deeply distressed if they have been champing at the bit to have sex, but then one of them is not so eager to engage in sexual intimacy come the wedding night.

Relax. This is quite normal. Anxiety and getting married are closely related, and anxiety and sex are not good friends! Fortunately, this stressful time will pass, and more relaxed times will arrive. Then the sex can improve. Don't make things difficult before then by traumatizing each other during a less than raunchy honeymoon.

Some people are worried that they must 'consummate' the marriage as soon as humanly possible. We suggest that this idea needs to be reconsidered, with the information we have been discussing on the nature of sex. You will most likely begin to have sex on your wedding night. Whether or not it includes intercourse ought to depend on what is the most loving way you can express your 'one-fleshness' at that point in time. If this means kissing and cuddling for a few days until you are relaxed enough to have intercourse without pain or fear, then we suggest that is a better expression of love and togetherness than a hurried and traumatic penetration before sleep on the wedding night. Remember, you are heading out on a lifetime of love (God willing); your wedding night is not your only opportunity to consummate your promises to each other.

Having said this, if you are taking it slowly and then find that you just can't help yourselves consummating things on night one—super!

5. Useful things to take with you

Another topic not often talked about before the honeymoon is the fact that to enjoy sex, a woman needs good lubrication. Under normal circumstances, the vagina provides its own lubrication (the 'wetness' that a woman experiences when sexually aroused). However, for various reasons—stress, anxiety, tiredness, medical problems, frequent intercourse—this natural lubrication may not be sufficient to ensure that sex is enjoyable.

For this reason, it is very worthwhile taking some lubricating gel with you on your honeymoon, as the above-mentioned conditions are common.

Note: using lubrication should not replace foreplay! It can be tempting for an eager husband simply to slap on some gel and get going, but this would be counter-productive. Certainly, you need to be kissing, cuddling, fondling and preparing for sex in the usual way—the gel is supplementary.

Using gel isn't an indication of sexual failure. Even the most relaxed wives can find that lubrication is not always easy. Even those who have been sexually active in the past may find that, on the honeymoon, they are not as naturally lubricated as they have been before (this is one possible side effect of the Pill). It isn't an embarrassment to use gel. It doesn't say anything negative about your sexual responsiveness. It isn't an indication that the husband is a bad lover and a disappointment. It doesn't imply that the wife is a cold fish.

Buy some gel. It's a good hurdle to surmount before the honeymoon. If you are anxious, it can make things so much easier. Even if you aren't, don't be proud. You may need it. You can get it in most supermarkets and certainly in chemists. And not all lubricating gels are equal—some are more similar to natural vaginal lubrication than others, so don't be afraid to ask a chemist or your doctor for advice. We highly recommend an Australian-made lubricant called *Wet Stuff* which is also hypo-allergenic and available in supermarkets and chemists— and a lot better and cheaper than fancy alternatives.

No matter how keen you are to have sex on the honeymoon, toss some gel into the trolley when you do the pre-wedding shopping. And just hope that you don't get a price check on it.

6. Sunburn, UTIs, gastro and thrush
Many good honeymoons are spent soaking up the sun's rays on a beach somewhere. This lovely, relaxing activity can come

at a deadly price for amorous honeymooners. That price is sunburn. There are few things less sexually arousing than a lobsterish back or bright red inner thighs. In fact, it is almost a contraceptive method, such is the lack of appeal of the sexual encounter to those suffering sunburn.

Take care to use sunscreens and hats, not to overdo the sunbathing, to spend time in the shade, and to keep yourself covered, if you want to enjoy sex throughout a beach-side honeymoon (and avoid melanomas).

Another common sex-destroyer on the honeymoon is gastro-enteritis (otherwise known as food-poisoning). Diarrhoea can really ruin a good time, and be especially awkward for newlyweds who may not be expecting such an assault upon their bliss. These ailments are especially common if you are holidaying in an exotic location where the food is unusual or the surrounds different from home. You can make provisions to cope with this, should it occur, by asking your doctor for some anti-nausea and anti-diarrhoea medications. It is best to be prepared, even if you end up not needing the medications, and especially if you are honeymooning a long way from doctors.

Perhaps the most commonly occurring problem on honeymoons is the urinary tract infection, a very painful problem which happens in women who have become sexually active. A urinary tract infection is a bacterial infection of the bladder. You get lower abdominal pain, fevers, pain on urination and a desire to urinate frequently.

There are two ways that a woman can contract this infection: i) insufficient lubrication during intercourse; ii) miniscule contamination of the urethral opening with bowel bacteria due to touching. There are some simple things you can do on the honeymoon, and subsequently, to help avoid this problem:

- Urinate quite soon after sex. This helps to flush out any invading bacteria. It is an important habit to learn, even though it might run counter to the romantic notion of curling up together and drifting off into blissful sleep after sex. The 'drifting off' experience is wonderful, but the grinding pain that can be visited upon the woman a day later is not. Having said that, we don't want women everywhere to become so paranoid that they are bouncing out of bed a moment after orgasm to make sure they avoid the dreaded UTI. There is no need to panic. In an ideal world, everyone has an ensuite where, after some post-coital cuddling, they can easily go to the bathroom and clean up a little, and just as comfortably slip back into bed and resume the blissful 'drift-off' experience. In the real world, it might require a little bit more imagination and tolerance.
- The honeymoon is a great time to commit yourself to drinking even more than your usual six glasses of water a day. When you visit the toilet after sex, have a drink at the same time (even if it means you are up to the toilet again later on). Drinking lots of water will keep your bladder filling up regularly, flushing out your urethra and removing any bacteria that could cause urinary tract infections.
- Use plenty of lubrication. As we have said, this is a key to ensuring a pleasurable sexual experience.
- Antibiotics. The best way to deal with UTIs, if (and, let's face it, when) they occur is to have some antibiotics ready to take. Antibiotics help your body to fight infections, and usually work within a few hours. You need to complete the course of medication to ensure that the bacteria do not return. Again, this is something your doctor can prescribe for you *before* the honeymoon. You just have

to ask. An important note regarding antibiotics and oral contraceptive pills: if you are on any oral contraceptive pill, the antibiotics can affect the pill's absorption, meaning it may not work. When on antibiotics, it is always recommended that you also use another form of contraception such as condoms to prevent pregnancy.

- One more irritating and potentially miserable medical problem that many women develop on their honeymoon is thrush. Thrush can occur when first entering a sexual relationship. It is not an infection, but an imbalance of yeast that lives in the vagina normally. It can occur particularly when you are on antibiotics. It is characterized by a thick, whitish vaginal discharge accompanied by extreme itchiness around and inside the vagina. This may embarrass one or both of you, but it need not. However, it will certainly slow you down sexually. Now that you are aware that it is a possibility, you can prepare yourself to avoid it or deal with it.

To deal with thrush when it occurs, it is probably best to visit a doctor and convince him or her that you would like a vaginal swab taken. Even though television advertisements suggest that expensive pills and topical creams will solve the problem, these may be unnecessary or in fact cause further skin irritation. You may need to find a chemist who still carries nystatin vaginal pessaries or cream. Your spouse will need to be thoughtful and sexually circumspect during your recovery, since vaginal intercourse at this stage really is out of the question. You need to get rid of the thrush first. Until then, you will need to consider other ways of being sexually intimate with each other—remember the joys of outercourse!

Summary

A honeymoon should be wonderful, relaxing, fun—the best holiday you have ever had. Unfortunately, it usually follows immediately after one of the most stressful, life-changing and emotional events of yor life—your wedding. It is also the end-point of the months of engagement, quite often a time of immense pressure and change. Dare we mention such things as in-laws, agreeing on a reception venue, financing the wedding and honeymoon, finding a new home, choosing a dress...?

For this reason, a couple needs to think of the honeymoon as also a time of *recovery*. It is an opportunity for you to wind-down from the wedding and all the planning that went into it. It is a time to slowly and gently bind yourselves together in the new state of marriage. The vows of the wedding service forged your union in the fire; now is the time for cooling down and letting the bond set solid.

The honeymoon is your first step into married life. Take it easy. Make it a low-stress, low-challenge experience. Just being together in marriage will be new enough without making the honeymoon itself into a grand mountain which must be scaled.

Chapter 9

The first year

Marriage is not something that you just sign up to and expect everything to fall into place. It requires devotion, even to the neglect of other things, if it is to become the happy, successful partnership that is envisaged. Once the decision to marry has been taken, the marriage itself must get a very high priority—especially in the crucial post-honeymoon stage.

The first year of marriage is also the time to get to know each other sexually. Make time for this. Don't just expect that you can both be working hard all day at your jobs, come home for dinner, and then jump into bed expecting everything to run perfectly. Setting up a good, godly marriage takes time and devotion. Fortunately, it is a very pleasant and attractive labour. Set aside quite a few weekends during the first year of marriage where you will have plenty of time simply to be together, doing something you like, and chatting about being married. Make sure you have time and place for the difficult conversations, whether they be about sex, money, unhappiness, anger, or anything else that could cause a rift between you. A good way to do this is to actually state it beforehand: "Darling, I'm feeling angry about something we talked about on the honeymoon. It will take a while to explain, so do you think we could go to the park on Saturday morning and chat about it then?" This is far more likely to become a positive experience for your marriage than starting to talk about the issue mid-week as your heads hit the pillow.

Talking about sex also requires time and place. And the time and place is not always the bedroom ten minutes before having sex! In fact, talking about sex and having sex do not always go well together. It is good to plan a time when you can talk freely about sex together.

People tend to have their thoughts backwards on sex and marriage. Generally, they are longing to get into bed together and can't imagine they will have any problems. We think things will start magically and perfectly, and go from there. It is much more likely that you will experience a few hiccups at first, and that your sexual relationship will grow slowly as you start to get to know each others' bodies and personalities, learn what pleases the other person, talk about your sex life and grow closer together. Your sex life will most likely be better some years down the track from marriage than it is when you set out—providing that you are paying attention to it.

We will now consider some aspects of sex in this first year of marriage.

Bread and butter position

Everyone is different sexually. There are certainly things we all have in common, but there are many differences.

A friend of ours, a radiologist, looks at x-rays of pelvises on a daily basis. She has commented on how remarkable it is that everyone's pelvis is different: different bone sizes, shapes, positionings. It is no surprise then that people enjoy different sexual positions. One enjoyable task to set yourselves during your first year of marriage is to find a 'bread and butter' position for sex.

Bread and butter—simple, nourishing, enjoyable and easy to make. Such is the kind of 'staple diet' that a newly wed couple would do well to discover together. At first read, this may seem unutterably boring. "We're going to have sex in a different way every night!", declares the young stallion. "Don't give me bread and butter; I want strange exotic fruits and caviar and freshly cooked lobster in a delicate white wine sauce!" More fool you, young stallion. You seem to be mistaking healthy eating for one-off feasting. An enjoyable sex life, sustainable during marriage, involves getting to know each other's basic pleasures; then you can add some nights of feasting.

The bread and butter position is the position in which you both enjoy sex the most. It is something you will have to discover, given the individual differences we have talked about. Not all sexual positions are enjoyable for all people, sometimes for physical reasons, sometimes for other reasons. You will need to talk as you explore these positions, telling each other what you enjoy and why you like it.

Following are some descriptions of the basic positions in which many people find sex enjoyable and comfortable.[2] We have tried to outline some of the things people report as

2. It can be difficult to find acceptable illustrations of these positions. We don't recommend books with photos because of the voyeuristic temptation. Instead, we recommend books with realistic line drawings (*A Celebration of Sex, Everywoman, The Joy of Sex*—be warned that the latest edition of this last title now contains photos instead).

enjoyable in each position, as well as some of the difficulties or objections people have raised. Remember: the point is not to become 'sexual superstars', able to swing from position to position like acrobats on heat. Rather, you are seeking a mutually fulfilling way of expressing your love and desire for each other. Nor do you need to progress from one position to another: it isn't a training course in having better sex. You may find that sometimes one position is preferable; at other times, you want something different. Try things out, without placing pressure on each other. You will slowly develop a 'sexual repertoire' which expresses your relationship.

Missionary

Husband on top, lying face down; wife underneath on her back.

This very popular position allows the man to penetrate deeply, to admire his wife's body and to look at her face. She, too, can see his face. It is, however, not always a position in which the wife is easily pleasured because her clitoris may not be receiving stimulation. It may be uncomfortable for the wife if the husband is heavy.

According to legend, Hawaiians were surprised to see missionaries making love this way, hence the name. It is unclear why or how they found out just what positions the missionaries used for sex, but the reputation of this position is that it is boring. Couples can come to their own conclusions, but there are variations of the position worth trying: wife wraps her legs around the husband's torso (penetration will be very deep); wife keeps legs closed tightly around husband's penis; wife rests legs on husband's shoulders (depends on leg length and husband's height!); husband rests on his knees rather than lying on top of his wife, and pulls her hips towards him now that his hands are available; wife lying, but near the edge of the bed, with her legs raised and her husband standing on the floor in front of her, holding her legs apart while he enters.

Kneeling wife

Wife on top, straddling his groin; husband underneath on his back.

This allows the woman to control the depth of penetration of the penis—a good thing, since deep penetration can be uncomfortable for her. The man enjoys great visuals and can use his hands to caress his wife. A variation is to have the wife leaning forward across her husband's face. This allows the man's hands to move behind to her buttocks, and changes the angle of entry of the penis, which some women enjoy.

A variation is to have the husband sitting in a chair and the wife sitting astride him or standing over him.

Side-by-side

Both husband and wife lying on their sides, facing each other. One has a leg over the other, to allow genital contact.

This is a very affectionate position, since the couple can cuddle and their bodies are very close together. Both bodies are supported, so no-one is trying a difficult balancing act. However, again the husband cannot easily touch the clitoris, which many women would like. Movement is restricted for both parties.

Crossed bodies

Husband on his side; wife on her back, with either one or both legs over husband's thighs.

This position allows the wife to be very comfortable, and gives the husband the ability to caress her and to use his penis in a controlled way. He can use his hand to guide his penis or stimulate his wife's clitoris. Thrusting is likely to be shallow. This position is popular during pregnancy.

Spooning

Wife lying on her side; husband lying behind her facing her back.

This rear-entry position is also popular during pregnancy, since the woman's stomach rests on the bed and she is well supported. The husband can caress her easily while having a very comfortable position for intercourse and control over the depth of penetration. Husbands often enjoy the contact of thighs to buttocks, too.

Wife in husband's lap

Husband kneels; wife also kneels in his lap, either facing him or with her back to him.

Again, the husband's hands are free to explore and to hold his wife as she controls the depth of penetration. There is a degree of athleticism required and it might be tiring.

Both kneeling

Woman kneeling; man also kneeling behind her, facing her back.

This is also a popular position. It is very visually exciting for the male, who can view his wife's genitals and his own contact with them. He can also use his hands to touch her, with a bit of balancing practice. The angle of entry for the penis is very different to frontal positions, which may or may not be enjoyable for the wife. A variation involves the wife lying on her stomach, with a pillow under her hips so that her bottom is slightly raised. The husband then lies on her back, or enters her from behind while balancing with his hands.

Standing

Husband and wife both standing, either facing each other or with the husband facing the wife's back.

Although not the position for extended lovemaking, it offers the potential for shower sex or rapid encounters. The hands of both parties are available and there is a good deal of control over entry of the penis. The height differential between the couple will be a factor in its success! A variation is to have the wife place one leg up on a chair or the edge of the bed, or to have the husband hold this leg. This enables easier access to the vagina and pulls the two bodies closer together.

This list gives you a good working knowledge of the many positions in which you can enjoy intercourse. Remember, sex is as much outercourse as it is intercourse, and good outercourse will help you in working out which positions are most popular for you. It will be a combination of where you like to be touched, what positions feel most loving, what position stimulates the clitoris or penis the best way, and how tiring or uncomfortable certain positions feel.

Sex need never become routine, if you are willing to enjoy experimenting with the possibilities of lovemaking. But your experimentation will probably lead you to a couple of positions that feel best and in which you both can enjoy sex much of the time. These are your bread and butter positions, and bread and butter is something you enjoy over and over again.

Talking about sex

Almost every cover of almost every magazine in the newsagent mentions sex (even the computer magazines). Most films are about sex in one way or another (yes, even Disney). Turn on the radio, and songs about sex greet your ears. Let's not even mention the music videos, which seem increasingly racy year after year.

Sexual language seems to flow freely from the mouths of everyone around us. And yet, within marriage, talking about sex with your partner is still difficult. It is a stumbling block in many a marriage, and one that is well worth overcoming as early as possible. In fact, the ever-present sexual noise in our society can make it harder to talk realistically, practically and personally about sex with your spouse. It can seem inadequate, as if you should both already know everything because every *Cosmopolitan*-reading teenage girl knows what it is all about, so you should too.

Of course, this isn't true. After a year of marriage, you will most likely know more about real sex than anyone who isn't married. Married people have sex more often than unmarried people, by and large; they also have more time for sex (i.e. longer periods of sexual contact); they are generally more relaxed about sex and therefore able to think clearly about it. There isn't much time to wonder about your partner's preferred style of foreplay when you are grappling with a stranger in a nightclub bathroom.

One of your best aids in talking about sex is a decent sense of humour. We use 'decent' deliberately, because there are damaging and coarse styles of sexual humour that will not help to build your marriage but will tear it down. We are not recommending these. Rather, we are recommending a lightening of the mood, a celebration of the earthiness and bodily nature of sex—the kind of humour that can giggle at the fumbling and rolling about that accompany healthy sexual play.

There's plenty to talk about. Here's a checklist of things you and your spouse might like to discuss:

When do you like to have sex?

What makes you want to have sex?

Where and how do you like to be touched?

What do you like to talk about during sex?

What sexual positions will we try?

What kind of contraception will we use?

Who will initiate sex?

Will we set particular times to have sex?

Will we set particular times not to have sex?

Before you are married, you won't know the answers to many of these questions, and you will only answer them by 'trial and error'. In fact, even if you have been sexually active before marriage, either together or with other people, you may find that the answers to these questions are not apparent until you have been married for some time. This is all the more reason to keep talking, to keep the channel of conversation open.

Did your family discuss it?

How did your family discuss intimate matters? Was it completely silent on them? Did Dad pronounce that the subject be dropped and that was that? Did your parents argue openly in front of you? Did your brothers and sisters joke about sexual matters and make you feel embarrassed?

It is likely that your family's way of discussing intimate matters will have affected your own approach to talking about them. It is worthwhile discussing this with your spouse or future spouse.

Words for sex

Part of the problem is finding the words to talk about sex. A couple has the great privilege of developing their own language to discuss sex. Some people use playful terms or popular slang; others prefer the proper medical or common names. It doesn't really matter what words you choose, as long as you do so together in a manner that is loving and that communicates clearly with each other. One of the wonderful things about a new family is the new language that evolves between its members. A husband can say to his wife, "If we can drong the boo-boos, I'd be very interested in mango salad, shuggy choppers" and have her join him in bed in no time. No-one else would have any idea what was being said, or have any response to it. The language is the secret language of the lovers, and one of the privileges of intimacy (and it doesn't have to be that silly).

These words will develop as you begin to talk about sexual matters. However, if you don't develop this language, you can find that you have been married for years and never really got very far in talking about sex. In order to get to the point where you can talk very specifically about what you do and don't enjoy in sex, you will lean heavily on these words.

Marriage should be a lifelong conversation, and the best marriages are those in which this conversation is sustained and enriched as the years pass. An important part of the conversation is talking about sex. Start out early with this. But don't expect it all to be sorted out on the honeymoon; this is a lifelong project. The point is to start the conversation, and continue it.

A few guidelines:

- Sex language must not be abusive, derogatory or filthy. The Bible has a lot to say about our language (Ps 19:14; Prov 10:31-32, 13:3; Luke 6:45; Eph 5:3-4; Col 3:8-10; Jas 3:1-12). Women often find slang terms to describe female genitalia to be crude and demeaning, so husbands need to work out carefully what language will demonstrate to your wife your respect for her body. Similarly, men can have their self-esteem attacked by careless references to their genitalia; again, talk together about what words you do and don't like.

- You may need to check with each other whether the words you are using are in fact the ones you still want to use. We know of a situation where the husband thought the wife enjoyed a more 'rugged' sexual dialogue, only to find out that she thought it was what he wanted and she had always desired something more delicate. He was very happy to change. Try to be honest with each other, not just doing what you think the other person wants. Honesty, not misplaced self-sacrifice, is the path to intimacy.

- Don't betray each other's sexual talk to outsiders. If a wife jokes to her best friend about her husband's words for his penis, she has betrayed their intimacy. If he finds out about it, he is unlikely to enjoy the same intimate sexual talk again. Even if he doesn't seem to mind, the exclusivity of your sexual relationship has been breached: don't let others into the bedroom with you.

What about talking during engagement?

People sometimes ask whether or not it is a good idea to talk about sex while you are engaged. The very godly motivation behind this question is the desire to avoid getting sexually involved with each other before you have in fact married. There is great wisdom in this resistance, for it is true that talking about sex with the person you love often leads to having sex. Intimate talk is a great turn-on, and those who wish to avoid it should do so. However, not everyone is going to feel this constrained or this aroused by sexual discussion. There are some things which it is very important to discuss before the wedding. In particular, it is important to discuss your attitudes to birth control. Without this discussion taking place, the wedding night could be a time of tension and fear.

For most people, the approach to marriage is accompanied by a growing openness about sex. This is very natural, and by and large will result in a happier wedding night and honeymoon. If the couple is taking care generally about their growing intimacy, then talking about sex should be part of the preparation for marriage. We have a few simple pieces of advice for making sure that talking the talk doesn't become walking the walk prematurely:

- Plan to talk about sex at particular times, rather than slipping into it when you are together anyway.
- Don't do this talking late at night, in a warm, cosy, comfortable, discreet environment. That is like putting a child under the Christmas tree and telling them not to squeeze the presents. Better to find romantically neutral venues, or venues where sexual play is unlikely.
- Work through a book together (such as this one), to keep your discussion focused.

- Perhaps mention to some of your other friends that you are now talking about sex and would like their help in remaining pure as you do. A good friend can regularly ask you how you are coping.

Sexual repertoire

We have begun to talk about this already. A married couple needs to develop their own 'sexual repertoire'. To do this, they need to be able to talk about sex, and to have explored the bread and butter positions that they enjoy.

The sexual repertoire includes far more than a list of positions in which intercourse is pleasurable. It includes, importantly, many of the activities that you may have done during your courtship: kissing, hugging, massaging, holding hands. These activities are all part of a sexual relationship, as we have already said.

It is important that as a couple you expand your sexual repertoire. By this, we don't mean that we all must end up hanging from the chandelier; rather you should always be interested in ways of increasing the intimacy between you. These 'increases' don't require courses in sex education or the purchasing of sex manuals. They should spring out of your relationship and the things you like doing.

You should be enjoying growing intimacy during this time of being newly-weds. You can't expect to leap head-first into the depths of intimacy on the wedding night. Your sexual repertoire will grow as you grow together in love, trust and confidence. Give yourselves a chance to develop this intimacy in an atmosphere of trust and acceptance, and not one of pressure or expectation or impatience.

For instance, you may think that it would be enjoyable one

day to touch your husband's penis, but at the moment that thought is too shocking to you. This may change over time, as you feel more comfortable with his body, trust him not to ridicule you, and overcome some of your anxiety about the male 'equipment'. And if it is something your husband desires, and he is willing to be patient about receiving it, he may find that eventually you are happy to do it.

Write down and lock in a drawer somewhere safely all the things that you like to do together. This will be a unique list to you as a couple, and you will add to it over time. When you have stale times, you can look back at the list and perhaps find some activity which rekindles your pleasure in each other.

Why do you need to expand your sexual repertoire? Why isn't it going to be satisfactory just to continue as you start out? There are a few reasons:

- Variety is important to sustaining your relationship. Like anything in life, repetition of one thing can lead to boredom and distraction. We need variety to stay interested. This may sound selfish, but it is a reality of the way our bodies and minds are made. If your sexual repertoire expands, there is always a new dimension of intimacy for you to explore.

  We need to emphasize here again that we are *not* suggesting that sex has to get kinkier and kinkier, or that a spouse has the right to force his or her partner into sexual activities that he or she is unhappy with, for the sake of 'variety'. This would hardly be loving, and the deepening and strengthening of your love is the issue at stake here. We are simply saying that sex need not— must not—become routine and boring, getting into a pattern where neither partner is particularly interested or aroused, but just going through the motions. Instead, sex should be playful, fresh, surprising, tender and fun. It will then play its role in strengthening your togetherness.

- The second reason that an expanding sexual repertoire is important is that, in order to develop one, a couple needs to learn how to negotiate. Negotiation—that is, talking about sex in detail and listening to your partner's needs and desires in order to come to a shared understanding of your sexual relationship—has to be one of the keys to an intimate and lasting marriage. If you are able to talk to one another about sex, you will be able to overcome a whole range of difficulties and incompatibilities. Conversely, if you find it difficult to negotiate, even small problems can become insurmountable.

Here's an example of a couple negotiating about sex:

Returning home after a night at the movies

Husband: "Gee that was fun. Let's get straight into bed when we're home!"

Wife: "Mmm. Yes! I can't wait to get my head on the pillow and go to sleep."

Husband: "Oh. That wasn't what I meant."

Wife: "Oh. I see. Um, well, OK darling. I'm very tired, but I don't mind if we have sex, as long as you just have a good time and I don't need to climax. I'm too exhausted for it."

Husband: "OK, darling. I hope you enjoy it a bit and surprise yourself! You are very generous to me."

How did you feel after reading that discussion? Did it sound like you and your spouse? Or did it seem a million miles from how you talk about sex? Did it offend you? Did you find it too frank, or did the husband seem selfish? Did the wife seem unfeminine talking in the way she did? Did you think there was anything wrong in the way they negotiated?

Talking about sex can be very difficult for some couples. It just doesn't fit with their personalities. But it is a *very important* skill to learn for a happy marriage. You need to learn to negotiate in this area, or it is very likely that your sexual relationship will suffer. However, the language you use should be your own language. You need to find words you are comfortable with, as we said earlier.

Here's another example of a couple negotiating:

Returning home after the movies
Wife: "I hope you're not feeling in the mood… are you?"
Husband: "Whenever I'm within a foot of you—you know that. Why do you ask?"
Wife: "I had a lovely time tonight, but I'm pretty exhausted."
Husband: "Fair enough… Would you stroke me while I masturbate, and kiss me a little? Is that OK? I'll do 70% of the work and you do 30%"
Wife: "How about 80/20?"
Husband: "All right…"
Wife: "It's a done deal!"

Negotiation ought not be too subtle, either. You need to ensure that you understand each other. This is why you develop a language of love which you can use to express things that are often hard to talk about. However, you still need to ensure that you are understanding each other, in order to avoid unnecessary complications. You may not need words, but you will need very clear signals.

A husband and wife met at a rodeo in a country town. Neither of them really liked rodeos, and they giggled together on that day and joked about cowboys and bucking broncos. Years later, when married, they developed a non-verbal language of love. When he is interested in sex, he puts on the cowboy hat she bought him as a joke that day when they met (sometimes it's only a cowboy hat, which makes his intentions even clearer). She notices this, and responds with a non-verbal signal of her own. If she puts on the perfume she wore on their honeymoon, it means "Yes, let's have sex"; if she puts on her flannelette pyjamas, that means "No". If she's wearing the flannies and her perfume, it means: "If you can convince me". The signals are clear, as long as the couple remembers what they mean to each other.

In our view, words are required and other signals can supplement the words. It's hard to find an appropriate symbol for "Tonight I'd love to have sex before our showers, as long as you don't rush me and we use a lot of gel". Words are the most articulate form of communication possible, so use their power to make sure you are really communicating about sex.

Masturbation and marriage

The Bible is silent on the subject of masturbation, but has plenty to say on sexual purity and sexual love. Masturbation fits into both of these categories. Before marriage, it can be used as a way of controlling sexual behaviour by offering an avenue of release that doesn't involve fornication. The difficulty, of course, is in controlling one's thought life while masturbating. A male who finds that he cannot masturbate unless he is thinking of something immoral (for example, another man's wife), should refrain.

It may be a surprising idea to think that masturbation need not finish with marriage. Instead, it can become part of a couple's sexual repertoire—part of the way they express their commitment to and love for each other. Let us explain.

When there is discrepancy between the sex drives of the husband and wife (most often, but by no means always, it is the husband who wants more sex), the couple might decide that it is OK for the husband to masturbate in order to have sexual release. He might do this while his wife is lying next to him: she may or may not participate in any way. Perhaps she puts her leg over his; perhaps she strokes his hair. Perhaps he is stroking her thighs as he touches himself. He is not creating a secret inner sexual world which excludes his wife; rather, he is enjoying sexual pleasure in the context of their companionship and emotional connection rather than their physical connection.

The big question relating to masturbation is fantasy. Does a married man or woman find it possible to masturbate using only fantasies of past or future encounters with their spouse? If not, masturbation is problematic. If so, it can be a useful addition to the sexual repertoire, providing variety, enabling the higher-drive partner to respect the lower-drive partner, and increasing the trust and love between them.

Chapter 10

Understanding the differences between men and women

Secular thinking goes through many fashions. It chops and changes, depending on which philosophies are prominent. Yes, science has made lasting discoveries. But even in science, the direction of research, the conclusions drawn from research, and certainly the way they are portrayed in the media, is dependent upon fashions.

Thankfully, we have the Bible, which is wisdom from age to age. From time to time, secular thinking catches up with Scripture, and one such area at present is the difference between men and women. There is currently greater willingness than in the previous decades to admit that women and men have profound and basic differences.

In Anne Moir and David Jessel's book, *BrainSex*, these researchers outline the genetic, hormonal and biolological causes of differences between the male and female brain.

When this book was being written, very few people thought it had any substance. Now, its arguments are much more widely accepted: men and women are hard-wired differently.[3] In fact, one of the bestselling books of any kind in the decade just past was a book that highlighted the differences between the sexes in its very title: *Men are from Mars, Women are from Venus.*[4]

This hard-wired difference results in some important differences about sex, in particular the motivation for sex. The basic difference in approach to sex can be summed up in a saying:

"Men have sex to feel good about themselves.
Women have to feel good about themselves to have sex."

Write this on a note and pin it to your pillow: it will be a great guide in understanding each other sexually. When a man has good sex, he finds it:
- relaxing
- unwinding
- self-affirming
- makes him feel potent
- fills him with confidence
- makes him feel loved.

After a hard day at work, a man might like to unwind with a round of sex. Without being at all unkind about it, he thinks that having sex would be a good way to ensure a peaceful night's sleep. He finds it hard to believe that his wife doesn't feel the same way.

3. Anne Moir and David Jessel, *Brain Sex: The Real Difference Between Men and Women,* Penguin, London, 1989.
4. John Gray, *Men are from Mars, Women are from Venus,* HarperCollins, San Francisco, 1992.

For women, the process is almost reversed. Before they feel like having sex, women need to have the feelings men *get* from sex. They need to:

- relax
- unwind
- feel affirmed
- feel confident
- feel loved
- wear something that makes them feel attractive.

This major difference in the approach to sex explains a number of common problems that couples experience. Men hope to jump in bed, have sex, then relax and go to sleep. Women hope to have an evening of chat, cuddling and relaxing, then have sex and go to sleep. This basic difference in male and female approaches to sex is the starting point for many other differences.

 ## An exercise for oldly-weds

Write down what aspects of your spouse you found sexually attractive *before* marriage. What qualities made you yearn for the intimacy of married life? After you have written down as many as you can remember, swap lists with your spouse. Talk about the lists and anything that is surprising.

Then give the list back to its writer, and write on them again. This time, write down the things that you still find arousing in your partner. Show each other.

How much overlap is there between the pre-marriage and today lists?

Men, women and desire

In the pages to follow, we shall explore the differences between the sexes in sexual arousal and sexual response. We can begin to see how important these differences are by examining two simple graphs.

1. *Male arousal over time in years*

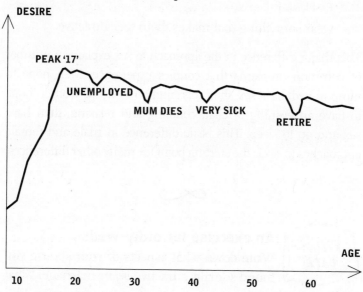

Under normal circumstances, men become sexually aware around 14 or 15. It is said that men 'peak' sexually when they are 16 or 17, but what this actually means is that this is the point at which they have maximum potential in sexual performance. They can achieve and maintain an erection very easily, and they can ejaculate and then recover quickly to repeat the experience. But these are hardly features of sexual maturity, so the suggestion that this is a man's sexual prime is useless.

As men get older, their physical abilities in sex—the ease

with which they achieve an erection, have an orgasm and return to sexual interest—decline slowly. However, for most men their *interest* in sex—their *desire*—remains reasonably consistent *throughout their lives*. The interest in sex is not dependent on the ability to have sex.

The saying that "sex is never far from a man's mind" is by and large true. There will be dips and peaks, but the graph of desire is a fairly horizontal one. There are things which put a man off sex, for instance, the loss of a job (a blow to his self-esteem and other identifying factors), a death in the family, a high level of stress in the workplace. However, the inhibiting power of these events is very short-lived for most men, who return to an interest in sex within days. In fact, some men will find that such events heighten their interest in sex, for reasons we shall explore later on. One couple told us the story of how they had lost a baby during the second trimester of pregnancy. The wife was distraught and felt listless and hopeless, but the husband wanted to have sex 24 hours later. She was thunderstruck, thinking him completely insensitive and a sexual deviant: how could he even think of sex, especially when it is so connected with having children? But the husband wasn't being bizarre; he was simply following the normal pattern of male desire, which is almost uninterrupted by life's events. He certainly wasn't connecting their sex with having a baby (perhaps we can admit that he was guilty of the first charge—insensitivity!).

The above story illustrates the difference we have summarized. The wife felt terrible, so sex was far from her mind. The husband also felt terrible about losing his child, but he wanted sex with his wife because it would make him feel better and show his love and connection to her, and he (wrongly) assumed it would make her feel better, too.

Story

Craig and Heather, both 29, have one young child. Craig has a job as a primary school vice-principal. Heather is also involved heavily at the school, working on the P and C. They have known each other since their teens and were virgins when they married. Craig rarely wants sex, making Heather very frustrated. He will not initiate it and when Heather does, he feels awkward and used. He can go for months without any interest in sexual contact. When Heather pursues him for sex, he backs off by finding more school work that needs to be done.

Their lives are very stressful and their relationship is time-poor. They need to prioritize their time and make school less important than their relationship. Some effort is required to separate work and home life. They need to find people to help at home with the little one. Craig needs some opportunities to relax *completely*.

There appear to be a number of possible reasons for Craig's lack of sexual desire. He may have a naturally very low libido; he may not be able to overcome his anxiety about sex in order to relax; he may be an over-achiever who never feels like his work is done and he is allowed to play. The first thing they are going to do is plan a two-week holiday in an environment where no-one can make demands on them (a cabin by an isolated beach). And they are going to spend some serious money to do it.

---

2. Female arousal over time in years

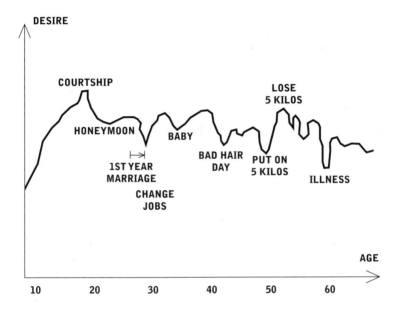

Women, generally speaking, take many more years to warm up sexually. Their interest and arousal tends to peak during the courting period, but their actual sexual performance seems to be highest in their mid-30s. It has been noticed in surveys and therapy that women become more sexually comfortable when they are in their 30s, and therefore report greater sexual satisfaction during those years. It doesn't necessarily mean that women get more desirous in their 30s. The benefit of this later peak is that, over time, women get to know themselves better, feel more relaxed about their bodies, become more in tune with their sexual responses and learn to enjoy sex more.

Female sexual desire is easily derailed. They can be much more easily distracted from sex than men can, and can be easily put off by things that happen before, during or after sex.

For this reason, it is in the husband's best interests that he learn what enhances his wife's sexual response—we shall come to this below.

Of course, we are describing activity across a normal range of women here. Some women will report greater sexual arousal over all; some will report low arousal. This spectrum of responses is normal, and doesn't necessarily indicate a sexual dysfunction that needs treatment.

Discovering enhancers and inhibitors

The names for these experiences which either increase your desire to have sex or put you off the idea are 'enhancers' and 'inhibitors'. An enhancer is anything that makes you feel more like having sex, and an inhibitor is anything which reduces the sexual urge. Within the marriage context, there are three easy steps to enjoying sex together:

1. Find out what your spouse's enhancers and inhibitors are.
2. Increase the enhancers.
3. Minimize the inhibitors.

Easier said than done. This is a much more difficult task than it first seems. It is discovered over a lifetime together. It involves talking, experimenting, talking again, relaxing, being honest, and then doing some more talking.

As we have seen, there are many differences between men and women over what makes them feel that sex is good. And we have also pointed out that you don't have sex with 'Woman', you have sex with one woman, your wife. She has her own desires and feelings and responses, and her own dislikes and fears and issues in the sexual arena. It is up to her husband (with her help) to get to know her in this way, and to enjoy the particular gift that God has given him in his wife. In a sense, the 'general enhancers' for women don't matter at all to a husband, except where they intersect with the specific enhancers of his wife. If a bunch of roses enhances 95% of women, but not your wife, don't even think of buying them.

Having said that, it still is possible to generalize about what a wide range of men and women find enhancing and inhibiting.

Women—enhancers

There are two enhancers worth mentioning that seem to get almost universal support from women.

1. Spontaneous acts of attention

This doesn't have to be expensive, but it shows that he is thinking about her. Running her a bath, occasionally lighting a candle or putting on her favourite music, buying her a gift— these are all sexual enhancers. They make women feel better about themselves, which makes them interested in sex. In fact, it is surprising to many men to find out that taking the garbage out without being asked is a sexual enhancer. Why is it an enhancer? It's because it shows that the man is paying attention; he is attentive to the couple or family's needs, and this generates sexual responsiveness in his wife. (Note that this doesn't mean she will be ready for sex every time he returns from pushing out the wheely bin. Rather, it means that she is more likely to feel positively inclined towards sex overall because she is thinking kindly of him.)

One sex therapist recommends '24 hour foreplay' to husbands who want their wives to be interested in sex. This sounds like enough to make any man celibate, but what it means is summed up in the phrase: pay attention to your wife. If the husband is aware of his wife's needs and wants—from what needs doing around the house, to the colours she likes, to the kid's birthdays, to when the next holiday is coming up— he is likely to have a more sexually responsive wife.

2. Time: the ultimate female enhancer

Time is one of the most valuable assets in a relationship. If you are just getting married, you will most likely be spending plenty of time together, doing things you enjoy, talking, relaxing, eating. This courting period is almost unique throughout life (in some situations, retirement approximates the courting period, and is sometimes experienced like a second honeymoon). However, after you are married, the pressures on your time together will grow very quickly. Work is the biggest pressure (housework included), followed by children. Very soon you find that you haven't spent time together alone all week. Under these circumstances, it is very unlikely that you will develop a healthy and happy sex life.

Time given to your relationship is time well spent. It will lead to a more active sex life. Men: if you want more sex, invest more time in the company of your wife. Time spent together allows intimacy to grow. How do you expect to gain the trust, confidence, admiration and excitement of your spouse if you aren't in each other's company?

Men—enhancers

First, a hint to women

Men's enhancers are an unpopular area of discussion currently, in both Christian and non-Christian circles. The male sex drive is viewed as insatiable and out of control—so why do we need to talk about male enhancers? Many wives say, "He's always on at me to have more sex. He doesn't need any enhancing!" Some men, mostly under 40, are also confused by a number of social changes which have made them uncertain as to whether they can in fact express their sexual desires, even to their wives. They feel that if they open their mouths to talk about sex, chances are they will say something that their wife hates and that will be the end of it. They are insecure about what valid masculine desires should be.

Women need to spend some time thinking about what it is that enhances male sexual response. This is difficult, because the *perversions* of male sexuality are around us everywhere in the form of pornography. Because women are almost always repulsed by this, they are unlikely to want to think about what it is in pornography that is attractive to men. There are evil desires which pornography taps into, but there are also good desires. (Please note: we are not in any way suggesting to women that they should get hold of pornographic material to research this subject. This book will provide you with the information that will help.) The good, God-given sexual desires which pornography exploits are listed below.

1. Visual displays of nudity, semi-nudity, apparent nudity, or even vague suggestions of nudity
This does not mean that a wife needs to mimic pornography. However, it does mean that in this area, a woman may need to act against her intuitions. Her intuitions tell her that her body isn't perfect, that her husband won't find her attractive, that her genitals are ugly, and that sex would be best with the light off. But the vast majority of men are fascinated by female genitalia, enjoy their wives bodies, are not as critical of them as she is, and would love to have sex with the light on so that

they can see as much as possible of what is going on!

A wife may take a very long time (possibly years) to change her view of herself in this way, but she needs to keep reminding herself of the way her husband is feeling about her. And he needs to lovingly remind her, too.

Let us again stress that this is something to *work on*, not something to try to revolutionize overnight. A wife who is shy or embarrassed about her body will need to be wooed and encouraged by her husband in order that she display it for him. The husband will need to learn to be patient, kind and generous, not criticizing and not pressuring his wife. At the same time, the wife needs to be courageous and generous, remembering that her body belongs to her husband as his does to her (1 Cor 7:4).

Take this one step at a time, and work within your own personality. If you aren't a red lace negligée kind of girl, you don't *have* to wear one. Think about what kind of nightwear you feel attractive in, and *ask* your husband what he likes. Maybe you are a cotton underwear kind of girl, and so is he! If he likes something that you feel completely uncomfortable with, then *tell him so*. Kindly, generously. If you can negotiate such things, you are well on the way to a happy sex life.

2. *Sexual initiative and enthusiasm shown by wife*
A common male complaint is that their wives aren't interested in sex, and never initiate sex. "I always have to make the first move", one husband said, "And when I do, I get a begrudging acceptance. Then she just lies there like a log while I do all the work. It's hardly worth it."

Men's sexual response is enhanced by the eagerness of the woman. One of the features of pornography that appeals to men is that the women are depicted as sexually eager, available and enjoying themselves. This gives a boost to the man's self-esteem—he feels sexually admired and sexually desired.

This poses a problem for the tired wife who is feeling unsexy and can barely muster the enthusiasm to let her husband touch her. But her enthusiasm for sex is a great gift to her husband. The key, of course, is for her own enhancers to be heightened. Then she will feel naturally more eager.

The problem of erotic focus

pillow talk

This has nothing to do with wearing contact lenses in bed, but it is an issue in sexual relations which is very common. It may be hard for engaged couples to imagine that during sex, one or both of the partners might lose interest in what they are doing, but it happens all the time. Believe it. Sometimes, a very simple distraction can deflate the sexual experience. For instance, the classic "Did you remember to put out the garbage, love" line from a wife to her husband in the middle of congress, is less joke than fact. Women often find it difficult to leave behind the everyday household tasks and give themselves over to enjoying sex. Likewise, men are often distracted by issues at work, by tiredness, or by other pressures. Of course, it can work vice-versa: a man may be wondering about shopping and a woman whether she closed properly on that business contract. Either way, there are plenty of distractions for those who are past the initial all-encompassing excitement of sex.

The responsibility in this matter is on each person to concentrate on what they have agreed to do. You have negotiated to have sex, so keep your part of the deal and focus! This is only polite. It may mean deliberately forgetting about the washing up that is sitting in the kitchen and needs to be done before bed. It may mean putting aside mentally all the worries and stresses of the day in order to enjoy this wonderful time of intimate relationship. It sounds simple, but it can be quite difficult for a person who is less than fully enthusiastic about sex. But, if you and your spouse have agreed to have sex, then lack of concentration isn't acceptable. It's plain bad form!

3. Novelty

There is a famous (most likely apocryphal) story about US President Coolidge and his wife, who were inspecting a government farm. Mrs Coolidge observed a rooster busily mating with one hen after another. The First Lady asked the attendant if this was normal; he replied that it took place over a dozen times a day. Impressed, Mrs Coolidge said, "Oh! Would you mind telling that to the President when he passes by?" When the President is told the story, he asks the attendant: "Does the rooster mate with the one hen over and over, or with different hens?" "Different ones, of course", the attendant replied.

And the President smiled: "Tell that to Mrs Coolidge when she passes".

There is no denying that novelty is arousing. There is also no denying that seeking novelty outside of the marriage is a disaster and a sin! Fortunately, there is great room for novelty within monogamy, and it is something which a husband (and a wife, to a lesser extent) finds enhancing. We have already suggested that you expand your sexual repertoire, and make it a lifelong interest to keep expanding it in loving, mutually satisfying ways. Sex which is more than bodily interaction need never be boring, since the combination of body, mind and emotions offers a great range of possible ways of loving each other afresh.

Here are some brief suggestions:

- Vary the length of time of intercourse. The occasional gift of a 'quickie' to the husband is very exciting.
- Pretend that you are not allowed to have intercourse, only outercourse, for a period of time (perhaps a week). Your excitement is likely to mount.
- Pay attention to parts of your husband's body that you don't normally caress.
- Use different lighting in your room for sex, and aromatic candles. Pamper your husband.
- As one of our very good older friends told us, "you can wear a different nightie every night of the week!"

Are you paying attention?

pillow talk

Men, did you get this? Although we have spoken generally about what enhances women's sexual responsiveness, you will need to find out what *specifically* enhances your wife. Some women like red roses, but not all. Some like being kissed on the neck, but some just find it ticklish. Some enjoy sitting together reading different books and not talking, but others will be brooding silently. You *must talk* about these things in order to serve her well.

Women, take note: let your husbands *know* what your enhancers are. Don't make him guess, and then resent the fact that he doesn't do what you would like. He is not a mind reader, and you are not in the business of making life difficult for him. Talk together about what you like. Be open, tell him exact details ("I love being given white chocolate—I just find it so creamy and gorgeous, as long as it hasn't got nuts in it"). If you like getting surprises, give him a range of very clear ideas about what you would like, and let the surprise be finding out which one he chooses. The key is communicating with each other and not leaving things to guesswork.

Inhibitors

There are plenty of obstacles to a happy, healthy sex life. Such is the intimate nature of sex that it is not very robust when it comes to suffering the slings and arrows of the sinful world. Our sexual desires are easily distorted and easily crushed. Some of these inhibitors are too large and specific for us to deal with at length. In Part IV we examine some of the terrible things that go wrong: child sexual abuse, pornographic addiction, violence and rape. But there are a number of less overwhelming, but still very debilitating, problems that prevent a couple from developing their sexual relationship. Some of the most commonly experienced ones are mentioned below. Since some apply equally to both men and women, we have not separated them.

Tiredness

Fatigue and sex are not bed partners. Although men will often trade sleep for sex, sleep deprivation tends to lower sex drive and decrease arousability. If you want to have more sex and better sex, make room for it in your schedule and don't overload yourself.

Physical illness or poor health

Sex drive is lowered when the body is not well. Aches and pains distract one from sex, as does weight gain and poor fitness. Prolonged or chronic illness may have specific effects on sexual arousal and performance. If you have a particular disease or disability, your doctor is likely to have literature about how it may affect your sex life.

Perfectionism

Sex isn't an activity where you can get 100%. Yes, you can reach for the sky and achieve a simultaneous orgasm with multiple waves for the woman, but even then you may not both be completely happy with the experience ("it could have gone on for longer..."). Because sex in marriage involves two people looking out for each other as well as enjoying their own sexual pleasure, perfectionists can find it very frustrating. Their husbands want it at inopportune times; their wives take too long to climax; it's messy; it's out of control.

In order to enjoy sex, a little less control is required. Both partners need to relax, to let things happen without worrying too much about how well or how quickly they are happening.

Losing a job

One of the few external factors which seems to lower the male sex drive is unemployment. It is an assault on the male esteem, in particular (females experience it, too, but it seems to be more damaging to the male sense of self).

Bereavement

Any grieving is an emotional drain on a person and may inhibit his or her sexual responsiveness. As mentioned earlier, men and women may respond differently to grief. Men may want to have sex in order to escape it; women may find this inconceivable.

Drug and alcohol use

Contrary to the talk on the streets, using drugs and alcohol does not heighten sexual responsiveness. Yes, a little relaxant such as alcohol can make a person less inhibited and more likely to want sex as a result. However, excessive use of alcohol leads to decreased vaginal responses, lower testosterone levels and erectile difficulties. Hard drug addicts are often sexually apathetic. And heavy smoking men often become impotent because it leads to the narrowing of the arteries in the penis.

Clinical (or endogenous) depression
This is a serious illness, not just a case of feeling rotten because of life events. Loss of interest in pleasurable activities such as sex can be an indicator of depression and may warrant a trip to the doctor to check things out.

Poor body image or self-esteem
Women in particular may find that the way they feel about their bodies puts them off having sex. This is a serious problem for both parties and requires attention. There are some brief points to mention here:

- Husbands tend to like their wives' bodies more than the wives do.
- Wear clothes that make you feel good, and even keep them on during sex if this makes you feel better.
- Losing just a little weight can make you feel a lot better. Set a realistic goal and a realistic time framework in which to reach it.
- 'Punch the inner critic'. When you catch yourself being self-critical, stop and say something positive about yourself instead.

The length of the penis

It's the joke of the millennium: size does matter. TV show after TV show has reinforced the idea that penis size is a measure of a man's prowess. It isn't, but that doesn't stop both men and women still using this idea as a psychological tool to make men feel inadequate. There isn't much a man can do about the size of his penis. Sure, there are medically dubious schemes and programs that the desperate male can waste his money on to try and increase the size of his member. But there is something else he can do without spending a cent.

If you are anxious about your size, take a look in the mirror. When you are standing front-on, you may feel it looks a little little. Now turn side on. That's better! The penis length is much more accurately viewed from the side. By and large, most men find this angle encouraging!

Remember, too, the variations in length depending on temperature and various other seemingly random factors!

Part IV

Early hiccups

Chapter 11

Common problems

There are some basic sexual problems that many couples experience early in their married lives. Amelia has found that people most often come to see her for treatment after the first year of marriage, having lived with the problem for that time. It is far, far better if you can attend to a problem as soon as it is recognized, so this section of the book aims to help you recognize some of the common hiccups that occur.

Vaginismus

This refers to spasms of the muscles low down in the pelvis, making sexual penetration very painful for the woman. It is an awful thing to experience, since it virtually prevents intercourse and causes both partners to feel fearful of sex.

It is, in fact, quite common. And the good news is that it can be treated in 100% of cases. It requires the assistance of a trained sexual health professional.

> ## Story
>
> Silas and Lisa were very controlled about sex during their engagement, even though they were both keen. Lisa experienced normal arousal—she was desirous of sex, her vagina seemed to lubricate normally, and she had been able to masturbate. However, on the honeymoon, things went from bad to worse. When Silas attempted to have intercourse with her she felt overwhelming pain and couldn't let him enter. They were both quite devastated by the loss of their honeymoon expectations, and it affected their relationship badly for the next six months. At that point, they saw a professional who gave them 'vaginal trainers'. These graded silicon cylinders 'train' the vagina to relax in order to allow the penis to enter. Lisa also followed a program of pelvic floor exercises known as Kegel exercises. Carefully, Silas and Lisa experimented with intercourse over a period of some months. They could eventually do it without pain.

Vulvodynia

This is the name of a poorly understood female condition that has only been identified properly since the 1990s and is now increasingly recognized. It can occur and recur anytime in a woman's life. It involves pain and discomfort in the vulval area which can feel like burning, stinging or pins and needles. It can be so severe as to cause secondary vaginismus or simply make intercourse, though possible, so unpleasant that it becomes repellant. The physical cause is not really understood and there are no real clinical signs, leading sufferers to be labelled as having a psychological problem with sex. Even if they don't have such a problem, the difficulties that this condition provokes for the relationship are enough to cause one!

There are some simple things women can do to 'treat' this unusual condition:

- avoid tight jeans, pantyhose, synthetic underwear and bike pants
- avoid soap and perfumed products on the groin
- avoid synthetic lubricants; use natural ones instead (e.g. saliva)
- increase water intake
- learn to relax the pelvic floor muscles
- some doctors may prescribe medications to reduce symptoms.

Unfortunately, all of these treatments have limited and unpredictable success. This condition is a great challenge to the sexual creativity and emotional resilience of the couple. We look forward to more research being done on this very common and complex problem.

Story

Harry and Jen had enjoyed a lovely, fun sex life for the first year of their marriage until vulvodynia (though not identified as such) came along and ruined everything. Suddenly, she had terrible burning pains in her vulva and could barely cope with intercourse. She went to several doctors, but no-one could find any medical problem. It was suggested that Jen might have a psychological aversion to sex. She couldn't think of one: did she have repressed memories of sexual abuse? Had she been faking her enjoyment of sex for the first year? Their relationship was strained to breaking point for six months as they tortured themselves looking for an explanation. However, they were both still wanting to be sexually intimate, and they made good use of outercourse to cope.

When they finally saw a sexual health professional, they were relieved to put a name to the problem. Jen was given a cream and some pills, but they didn't seem to help very much. They remain unable to have intercourse, although they have found a bread and butter position for mutually satisfying frottage (rubbing). They are pursuing other programs of experimental treatment and feeling quite desperate about the fact that nothing much is improving.

Erectile dysfunction

This common problem affects most men at some point in their lives, even if only for a brief time. It refers to the inability to get and/or maintain an erection for long enough to have sex. It can be humiliating and disappointing for all involved, and this embarrassment can further compound the problem. It can also cause a woman to doubt her attractiveness and desirability to her spouse and put great pressure on a relationship.

When younger men (say, under 40) experience erectile difficulties, the primary cause is usually a psychological issue such as performance anxiety. Performance anxiety refers to a concern that you are "not doing things correctly"; you start to worry that you are being judged or assessed. This anxiety causes a physiological 'fight or flight' response, diverting blood from the penis and to the muscles, heart and brain.

Sometimes, the causes of erectile dysfunction are physical. As men get older, the chance of a biological reason for erectile dysfunction increases. Diseases such as diabetes and arterial disease may affect this area. A doctor should assess such things.

But, by and large, erectile dysfunction is a psychological

issue. It sounds counter-intuitive, but getting an erection is easier when you are relaxed. If he is relaxed, and there are no physiological issues, a male can maintain an erection even when he is quite old (although it may be less firm and upright).

If you experience an erectile problem, the news is in fact very good. It used to be the case that you had to undergo numerous embarrassing physiological tests, but that was then and this is now. Just occasionally, a medical treatment comes along which almost totally solves a problem. PDE5 inhibitors are one such miracle; you will know them by their drug names such as Viagra, Levitra and Cialis.

This medication ensures that blood flows to the penis when sexual excitement occurs, and stays there in order to maintain a firm erection. It's taken as a pill, a short time before intercourse. Before taking it, you do need to consult a doctor to check that it will be safe for you and won't interact with any other medications you are on.

The success that this medication brings can also boost the man's confidence, thus addressing some of the psychological issues.

A man may find that erectile dysfunction is context-specific, that is, it only occurs in certain situations. If this is the case, it will be very important to discuss with your spouse why this might be so. This may be a difficult thing to do, but it is an important step towards solving the problem. Talking about it may break the cycle of embarrassment, nervousness and fear of failure. It may also uncover bigger issues related to sexual arousal, sexual orientation or previous sexual experience. Although very painful to discuss, honesty and openness are the way forward.

It is good to know that in most cases, there is a positive solution to erectile dysfunction.

'Premature' ejaculation

Premature ejaculation refers to the male climaxing earlier than expected or desired. This ranks highly on the male anxiety scale: Am I a premature ejaculator? What is premature? Is it permanent? What can I do about it? The anxiety caused by this subject can in fact be self-fulfilling, since anxiety about sex and premature ejaculation are often related.

The truth about premature ejaculation is that there is no definition of what it is. As we have repeatedly said, it is a matter for the couple and the couple alone. No-one can tell you how long intercourse should last before ejaculation; there is no optimum amount of time. Your sexual relationship as a married couple is what matters.

In a lot of cases, a husband or wife may feel that the husband is a premature ejaculator because the wife takes longer to reach orgasm than he does. But this is a premature judgment: there are plenty of other ways to understand such a situation. Let's tease out this subject.

- It is a myth that a man and woman must have simultaneous orgasms for sex to be mutually satisfying. Many couples may desire and pursue this as a goal, but many others will be happiest with other outcomes.
- Before labelling a man as a premature ejaculator, explore the possibility that the woman needs longer to become excited than the couple is allowing. The wife may be stimulated manually or in other ways until she is on the brink of orgasm, when her husband enters her and they both climax. The actual time of intercourse might in fact be very short, but both partners can be completely satisfied.

Having said this, it is true that there is a common problem whereby men climax earlier than either they or their wives desire. It is also an episodic problem throughout a man's life. When boys are growing up and masturbating, this is often done furtively, quickly and in a flush of guilt. Whatever we may think of this, it has effects on the male progress towards orgasm. It tends to become a very uncontrolled process, rushing from arousal to orgasm as quickly as possible. There is no time for gradually building up a sexual response, pausing, or controlling the activity. This has detrimental effects for a man entering a sexual relationship with a woman. This fast-track approach to sexual activity may transfer to their activities together, making it very difficult for the man to enjoy sex at a pace acceptable to his wife.

A husband may need to 'unlearn' his approach to sexual excitement and arousal. He needs to slow down and enjoy elements of sex that he may previously have ignored. For instance, he may need to focus more on his wife than his own sexual response. He may need to 'dethrone' sex in his mind in order to quieten his body's responses.

Some experiments for men wanting to slow down:

- Wear a condom to reduce penile stimulation.
- Relax before sex. Take a bath (alone!). Read quietly. Go for a walk. Don't even think about sex until you are in bed together.
- Agree that you will touch your wife, but she won't touch you during foreplay. Arouse her in whatever ways she enjoys, focusing on her pleasure and your interest in her. Don't think about your own pleasure. In fact, leave your clothes on while you do this.
- With your wife, or alone, practise being touched sexually without going on to orgasm. For instance, your wife

might stroke your penis for a couple of minutes every half hour over one evening, but not move towards intercourse. In this way, you learn to be aroused without rushing straight to orgasm.

- Enjoy extended 'non-sexual' touching, by which we mean touching, cuddling, caressing parts of the husband's body other than his genitals or other areas that he finds exciting. For instance, the wife might give him a back massage with his shirt off. The aim here is for the husband to get used to having his body touched without it leading to intense arousal.

- Have sex more often. Negotiate with your wife so that you have sex twice a night for a few nights. The first night, have intercourse and climax quickly. Then set about pleasuring your wife and have intercourse again that same night (you may need to wait a few hours). Do the same thing the next night, and the next, and you may notice that the duration of intercourse before ejaculation begins to increase. Please make sure you have satifactorily negotiated this arrangement, and both parties are happy about it!

- Have 'non-visual' sex, that is, where the man has no visual stimulation. Turn off the light; close your eyes; block out any mental images that come into your mind. Instead, focus on purely physical sensations.

There are some cases of premature ejaculation which will require higher level medical intervention. If you are still having problems after trying exercises such as these, consult your local doctor.

Rigid thinking

Beware of rigid thinking in marriage and sex. Clear thinking is good; pure thinking is good; correct thinking is good; but rigid thinking leads to disasters. By rigid thinking, we mean ideas that are set in your mind with no biblical, relational or logical reason for them to be there. One such rigid thought might be this: my father always told me about how great his wedding night was; I have to have a great wedding night in order to prove myself to him. Here's another: if I don't bring my wife to orgasm, I have failed her sexually. Here's one more: sex anywhere other than the bedroom is risqué and dirty.

It is amazing how many such thoughts clutter our minds and prevent us from improving our situation.

Anorgasmia

This simply means the inability to have an orgasm. It is more often a problem with women than men. It is a common joke that the female orgasm is an elusive beast, produced only under controlled laboratory conditions with highly skilled sexual technicians involved. And, to some degree, this is true! Whilst most men find that the path from excitement to arousal to orgasm is a pretty direct one, women often find it much more circumspect. They can become excited and aroused, but by no means be certain that the sexual experience will lead to an orgasm. Furthermore, the orgasm itself is a many and varied thing for the woman, whereas one orgasm is more often quite similar to another for the man (all things being equal).

MAN   WOMAN

The female orgasm can seem like the holy grail to those who find it difficult to achieve (and to their husbands). It can seem as if it is a sexual failure not to have an orgasm, or to be able to bring your wife to orgasm. This is not the case. There are many reasons why a woman may not be able to have an orgasm. These include:

- intense anxiety on her part
- past sexual abuse
- fears related to sexual pleasure e.g. inappropriate guilt, selfishness
- insufficient lubrication
- wrong kind of stimulation (too strong/soft/direct/indirect/etc)
- inability without a physiological basis. 10% of anorgasmic women are never diagnosed with any specific problem.

Story

Julie, a 40-year-old woman, presented for treatment to a sex therapist after 18 years of marriage. She had never had an orgasm and decided that this was something she wanted to pursue. She was having satisfactory relations with her husband, but now her children were older, she was rediscovering her relationship and their marriage. She thought it would be good for their marriage if she could become orgasmic. Her husband supported the idea, but was not happy to receive any professional support himself.

Julie was given reading material, vibrators, pelvic floor exercises and self-examination exercises, and pursued this enthusiastically. Her husband has begun to show increased interest in sex, and they both feel happy that they are once again focusing on their relationship in this way. Eighteen months have passed since Julie's first visit, and the results are still pending.

Although the lack of a female orgasm does not mean that a couple is a sexual failure, it can mean that their sexual relationship is not satisfactory. Some couples are in fact content that the wife does not orgasm, but there are many more couples who long for this experience of shared intimacy and look for ways of changing the situation.

Fortunately, there are plenty of ways forward for the anorgasmic woman.

1. Experiment

The first step in the relationship is to experiment with sexual activities together in a comfortable context. This is an issue which the couple need to embrace *together*, rather than identifying it as 'the wife's problem'. Using the ideas in this book—developing a sexual language, adding to your sexual repertoire, finding time for intimacy—is a way to find new approaches to the sexual experience which might change the situation and lead to orgasm.

A note on 'relaxing': it is very common for counsellors to tell anorgasmic women to relax, and it is certainly an important thing to suggest. However, it can be counter-productive. The experience of orgasm is, in fact, a very intense and 'unrelaxed' experience in which the body reaches a heightened state with many muscles straining and chemicals racing. The advice to relax can sometimes decrease arousal and derail the journey towards increasing pleasure. For those in this situation, perhaps a better way to think is to have 'erotic focus'. We discussed this earlier on: focus on the 'sexiness' of sex, its physical nature, its smells and tastes, its 'escape the everyday world' opportunities. To have an orgasm, one needs to be abandoned to the sexiness of the sexual experience—the sensations, the fact that you are in a relationship where you can be sexy, the exclusive wonder of it all. If you can do this— without it increasing your anxiety—then you may make progress. If erotic focus instead makes you anxious and nervous, then perhaps the best advice to you is, in fact—relax! (You ought also to discuss why this is so with someone.)

2. Train

If sexual experimentation with her husband doesn't bring a wife to orgasm, she may need to go into training. This can take place at several levels. The first is to start to touch herself, look at herself and discover how her own genitalia respond. Very often, women with anorgasmia have not masturbated and may not understand their own anatomy very well. This is a hurdle they need to overcome. In the privacy of the bedroom, with or without her husband, the woman can use a mirror to look at herself, touch her labia and discover what it is exactly that she has down there. She may be able to determine what parts of her genitals respond to touch, which bits are hypersensitive, and which bits don't respond at all.

Or so it may seem. Female responsiveness changes as sexual response grows—what feels good at stage one may feel dull at stage seven. What felt awful at stage two becomes exquisite at stage six. It can be very confusing for all involved! But this is the way God has created women: complex, diverse and multi-layered. Most women have one or two ways in which they can orgasm. Most need to feel very safe and secure in order to achieve orgasm. Sometimes, they may need external assistance such as a vibrator or oral sex or manual stimulation. 30% of women can climax through intercourse alone; 40% need their husbands to stimulate them in other ways as well; and 20% need to stimulate themselves.

Story

Lindy had become a Christian in her late 20s. She had had multiple sexual partners through her adolescence and had concluded that she was anorgasmic. She had been happily married to a Christian man for two years and her lack of sexual responsiveness had not changed. However, the couple had not experimented with sexual positions because she felt that this was part of her pre-Christian life. After much discussion, it was decided that she and her husband would talk about a sexual repertoire that they would enjoy as their own. After some enjoyable experimentation, Lindy found that she was in fact orgasmic in certain sexual positions and with the gentle manual attention of her husband to her clitoris. A review was also made of her medication, and it was found that anti-depressants may have been suppressing her orgasmic ability.

Further discussion with her counsellor helped her to understand what in fact an orgasm was. Lindy had developed a view that it was a miraculous feeling from head to toe. It was explained that this was not always the case; rather, orgasm was a desire for sexual intercourse which reaches a point of intensity and then resolves over the next 30 seconds or so. It was certainly vastly pleasurable, but it wasn't the ecstatic otherworldly experience that Lindy had imagined.

pillow talk Women's genitalia

Young girls (in fact, women of any age) are discouraged from appreciating their genitals. They often hear grotesque jokes about how funny they look and how bad they smell. Who feels like being vulnerable or enjoying (or letting someone else enjoy) what seems so full of embarrassment and shame? If men want to enjoy women's genitalia, perhaps they need to stop giving out mixed messages and appreciate them.

There are more sexual problems that we could mention, but these are the most commonly occurring for the couple who are entering into a sexual relationship. If you are concerned that you may have a problem such as these, first talk to each other about it. Then you can agree to seek some help from people who know how to take steps towards improving the situation.

Chapter 12

Things that really do happen to Christian couples

We suspect people's reactions to this part of the book may split in two directions. One is to be baffled and confused that these subjects need to be discussed in a book on sex in marriage for Christians. Doesn't everyone know these things are wrong? Why are you making me blush by including them in the book? Do we really need to talk about them now?

Another group of people will react quite differently. They will have exhaled heavily and sighed to themselves: "Phew! At last someone has acknowledged it". It is to this second group of people that this last section of the book is addressed. We hope to provide some sane and compassionate thoughts for those who are caught up in one of the following sexual distortions. However, we do hope that the first group of people —the baffled and confused ones—will read on, too. For he who thinks he stands, take heed lest he falls. Sexuality and passion are difficult to fetter, and many unpredictable and surprising circumstances await God's people around the corners of life. If you think you are beyond the grip of such things, you deceive yourself. Jeremiah was right: "The heart is deceitful above all things and beyond cure…" (Jer 17:9).

Furthermore, Christians belong to the people of God, the family that we call 'church'. Even if these matters do not touch us personally, we may need to offer help to our friends and congregation members. It is important that we treat sexual sins seriously, not only by condemning them but also by attempting to understand them and help people escape them. These sins trap people in terrible situations, causing them great suffering. Their cause is tied up in sin, but it is not always the sin of the individual with the problem (for example, sexual abuse and, arguably, cases of homosexuality).

Our approach to these matters needs to be fourfold:

1. Understand the teaching of the Scriptures on the matter.
2. Condemn wrong behaviour and champion right behaviour.
3. Take practical steps towards changing sinful behaviours, probably involving some professional assistance.
4. Pray and bring these matters before God.
5. Have compassion for those affected.

We have mentioned taking practical steps before prayer for no reason other than to emphasize that practical steps *will need* to be taken to overcome these situations. We sometimes hear of Christians who are averse to doing anything labelled 'counselling', 'therapy' or 'treatment', because they want to trust in God alone to relieve them of their problems. This is not Christianity; it is superstition. God works in and through those around us to bring about his purposes. He does not, in the usual course of events, transform people overnight in response to prayer. Of course, he can and does do this. But, in his sovereign wisdom, it is more often the case that God provides the resources to help people from within their families, their churches and their communities—often even using the skills of secular practitioners such as social workers, psychologists, psychiatrists and doctors. We have laboured this point because it is too often resisted by Christians who want to do the right thing. Let us state it plainly: going to a doctor or a therapist can be the right thing to do as a Christian (even a non-Christian doctor or therapist).

In recent times, some Christian psychologists (Larry Crabb is one of them[1]) have suggested that Christians have taken on board a therapeutic culture which no longer trusts that God gives the church the abilities to counsel its members through the Scriptures and prayer. This is an important point, but in the Australian context it is not the problem we have encountered. More often, the problem is a resistance to using 'techniques' at all.

If the five steps above are taken, we will be utilizing all the resources that God has given us in order to try to live in a manner that is pleasing to him. And we are going to need all of these resources, for the problems that we deal with below are extremely challenging to any relationship. Most of them will not be easily or quickly remedied; they will be ongoing issues for those involved for their whole lives. They are the outcome of entrenched sinfulness in the world, and part of God's judgment upon the world. If they describe your situation, may God grant you the wisdom, strength and

1. Larry Crabb and Kevin Dale Miller, 'Putting an end to Christian psychology', *Christianity Today*, 14 August 1995. Reprinted in *The Briefing*, #185, 20 August 1996, Published Abroad supplement, pp. iii-iv.

endurance to bring about the changes required. And may you be certain of his love and acceptance through the faithfulness of Jesus Christ, who took our sins upon himself on the cross, that we might be seen as pure and radiant in God's sight.

Homosexuality

Homosexuality has been the focus of an incredible amount of attention over the past three decades. It has been researched and reported at great length in scientific circles, as well as featuring prominently in the fields of entertainment. It is now uncommon to find a television sitcom which *doesn't* feature a gay character, such has been the movement of the gay world into the mainstream of Western culture. The gay character is very often the most appealing one, too.

Although much research has taken place and many reports been presented, there is still little consensus over the causes of homosexuality. Some groups suggest a genetic predisposition (as with almost any condition); others insist that it is a choice made entirely without physiological origin. The fact is that at present there is no way of saying anything conclusive about the causes of homosexuality.

One feature on which there is some consensus is that people who express homosexual desires have usually experienced some kind of disappointment in their relationship with the parent of their sex; that is, a son with his father or a daughter with her mother. This disappointment might be in the form of domestic violence or sexual abuse, or it could be of an emotional nature, such as the oft-discussed 'absent father' syndrome in homosexual men. In some way, the relationship with the parent of the same sex is damaged.

We mention this connection because it is potentially important for dealing with unwanted homosexual feelings.

There are two forms of homosexuality: men who have sexual relations with men, and women who have sexual relationships with women (lesbianism). The two forms have some similarities, but are actually quite different. We will not deal with the details here, but consult the reading list if you wish to investigate further.

Story

Walter, a 23-year-old man felt that he was homosexual in orientation and was unhappy about this. He longed to reorient, and was happy to accept that this would take a very long time. He had some classic elements in male homosexuals: his father was a travelling salesman who was cold and distant when he was home (only on Saturdays). He also reported that, starting when he was 10, a neighbour had forced him to touch his penis for a period of years.

Walter appeared to be a very measured, pleasant man, but was in fact extremely angry about what had happened to him. However, his anger had not been expressed; instead, he felt only guilt for something that was not in fact his fault.

He is learning to express this anger. He is also learning to accept that he should have had better male role models, but this world is fallen and that does not always occur. He is working on appreciating the female form and femininity, but progress is slow and uneven. He is interested in marriage, but his counsellor is recommending that he does not rush towards this goal.

It can occur that a married couple discovers at some point in their relationship that one of them is, or has always been, attracted to members of their own sex. This is a potentially devastating realization for both spouses, although it does not mean that the relationship is automatically doomed. Has the homosexual attraction led to homosexual sexual activity (i.e. sex outside of the marriage)? The answer to this question will help the spouse to understand what degree of deception has been involved. From here on in, the spouse will require *total disclosure* if any sense of trust is going to be re-established. There are Christian organizations, such as Liberty Christian Ministries, who can help with the issues surrounding re-orientation (see the reading list for details).

There is another dimension to homosexuality which is not often discussed. Some men do not identify themselves as homosexuals, but will pursue sex with men. At first read, that sounds like nonsense. But what it means is that some men, whose sexual orientation is plainly heterosexual, will also engage in sex with men. Clearly, this is wrong behaviour for a Christian, married or unmarried. It more properly fits under the heading of sexual addiction, for it represents a man who is so sexually driven that he will jeopardize his marriage for further sexual experiences.

In this situation, repentance is the first requirement. After that, we strongly suggest individual and couple therapy to explore the issues involved. The husband must unlearn this perversion of his sexual desire in a similar way to unlearning pornographic addiction or any other type of sexual activity outside the marriage. The situation is dire, but not hopeless. Change is possible.

Sexual abuse

Sexual abuse is any behaviour, attitude or verbal response from an external party that interrupts normal sexual development. Those who have suffered sexual abuse often find it difficult to begin or maintain healthy marital sex lives. They are unsure about sexual identity, sexual boundaries (What is my partner allowed to do to me? When can I say no?) and valid sexual feelings. Children who have been sexually abused often feel guilty and ashamed, even though they are the victim. A child is never responsible for his or her sexual abuse.

Victims of sexual abuse who marry are very likely to need a great deal of empathy and patience from their partners. Their experience of sex in marriage will be tainted by, and mixed up with, their memories of abuse. This may express itself as a loss of interest in sex, or in physical dysfunctions that affect sex (for example, the inability to maintain an erection). The couple will need to distance the sexual abuse from their own sexual relationship in order to overcome its influence. Remind each other that the problem relates to something that happened in the past, not to something between each other.

There are a number of false ideas that recur in sexual abuse victims. These can all be talked through as a couple in order to try to reshape the thinking of the victim in the area of sex. They are such ideas as:

- people cannot control their sexual urges
- sex hurts physically and emotionally
- sex is a bargaining tool
- sex is shameful and needs to be kept secret.[2]

2. This list is based on Rosenau, p. 325.

As with everything in marriage, talking about abuse is a powerful way of countering its power. Talk positively together about how special your sex life will be and how wrong it was that one of you (or both of you) suffered abuse in this way. Along with such talking, you may consider seeking professional counselling in some cases.

Story

Susan, a 22-year-old woman had been going out with Denis, whom she thought of as her best friend. They were talking about marriage. However, she felt no sexual attraction towards Denis. She became concerned that something was wrong with her sexual response and sought professional help. During discussion, it arose that an older female neighbour had exposed her breasts to Susan while babysitting when Susan was 10, and had coaxed Susan into taking off her clothes and kissing the woman's breasts.

Susan had pretty much forgotten this, and didn't believe it could jeopardize her responses years later. She wasn't sure it should be called sexual abuse. However, her current sexual problem suggests that it certainly was, and that it did affect her.

Bravely, she told her boyfriend; it turned out that he too had been sexually abused. They have begun to talk about what happened to them, and to distance their own relationship from the sexual events of the past. They are finding the experience painful, but they are feeling close together and looking forward to the future.

Transvestism

Firstly, many people don't think that this exists. It is a fantasy, something that raises a laugh in the *Rocky Horror Picture Show*, but is unlikely ever to be a problem in Christian contexts. This just isn't true. Although it would not be labelled common, it is certainly seen often in any community, and Christians are not exempt. It is also often mistaken for homosexuality. There is a wrong idea that homosexuals by definition enjoy dressing up in the clothing of the other sex and that male homosexuals feel like females. However, transvestism is a separate sexual perversion. We need also to distinguish it from people who feel like they are in their deepest being the opposite sex to how people identify them. This is a particular phenomenon known as transsexualism and it usually begins fairly early in life, often before the age of five. It needs to be examined quite differently to transvestism and should be referred to a doctor. It may or may not involve any sexual sin.

Transvestism is a perversion of sexual arousal and sexual identity which commonly manifests itself in heterosexual men. It doesn't mean that the man identifies himself with women, nor that he feels arousal towards men (but sometimes he will). Rather, it has to do with the things which arouse him sexually. These are complex issues, and some transvestites and transsexuals are of homosexual orientation. The message is that these sorts of compulsions do occur among Christians, and need to be approached with compassion and a resolve that it must change. Again, professional help is recommended.

Chapter 13

Be prepared

We hope that Part IV, indeed the whole book, has not been frightening to those approaching marriage. We certainly don't intend it in this way. Rather, we hope that it offers some relief to those who are, or have been, affected by any of these distortions of sexual behaviour and identity. We hope it represents the first step to making changes: acknowledging that there is a problem. We also hope that it offers some fortification against these problems for those fortunate enough to have avoided them thus far.

A great many marriages will survive and flourish without having to deal with any of these terrible circumstances. However, enough marriages will be affected by them to make it important that all marriages give some consideration to the problems others may face.

Can we leave you with a few thoughts on coping with the possibility of sexual trauma and sin in the context of your marriage?

- Your sexual union needs protecting. It will be challenged and attacked on any number of different fronts. The best form of defence is attack—so to speak. If you are positively pursuing your sexual relationship, learning to enjoy and cherish and honour each other in it, then you will be building up barriers to any assaults that might come upon you. It is for this reason that it is so important to *talk* about sex as a couple, and in other fellowship situations. We must take seriously the possible threats to our marriages and do all we can to nip them in the bud. Invest time, money and energetic focus in your marriage.

- What can seem outlandish, revolting and impossible can also become ordinary, everyday and even comfortable. If you read this section thinking that it is worlds removed from your situation, that is wonderful. However, after years of marriage, it may not seem as distant as it first did. The difference between revolt and comfort might be only time and opportunity. Do not be naïve about the sinfulness of the human heart (especially, it must be said, the male heart) in the sexual arena. It is best to accept the possibility of everything, in order that everything bar faithfulness be resisted.

- Christians must remember that our relationship with God is built on forgiveness and faithfulness. God forgives us for our extraordinary disobedience, a disobedience which the Bible often describes as 'unfaithfulness'. In our unfaithfulness, God remains faithful to us and does not abandon the relationship. Our marriages must also be built on forgiveness and faithfulness. We do not promise in the wedding service never to sin against our spouse (if only we could make such a promise); rather, we promise to remain faithful to them, to stand by them, for better or worse.

A final word

or those who are reading this book before getting married, we hope it helps you start down the path towards a godly and fulfilling sexual relationship. We have tried to spell out some of the basic (and less basic) aspects of beginning your lives as 'one flesh'. It is at once a deep mystery and a very practical, physical, day-to-day reality. We need a view of sex that is simultaneously high and low—lofty in its view of the sanctity of the marriage bed (see Heb 13:4), and down-to-earth about the joining together of two bodies for mutual pleasure and expression of love.

We have been frank about the realities of sex in a sinful world. Sexual sin is a source of great pain for a couple, newly wed or otherwise, but it is not an insurmountable obstacle for those who are committed to each other and to the forgiveness found in the gospel of Jesus Christ. We have not been able to deal in detail with the real and practical issues of dealing with sexual sin, but we hope we have provided enough information and guidance to begin down the path to recovery and godly intimacy.

In sex, God has given couples a generous, delightful and extraordinary means of sharing for this life. It is something that is worth dwelling on in our marriages, worth studying and reflecting on and 'pillow talking' about, rather than merely performing in silence with the lights out. The erotic love poetry of Song of Songs and the exhortations of the apostle Paul encourage us to be open, honest, sensual and devoted about our sexual love. This may not be easy for some Christian couples, for all sorts of reasons of cultural background or personality, but it is a part of marriage that we should not ignore. There are God-given pleasures there to be had for each and every married couple. Again, we stress that the point is not to become sexual giants, but to increase your intimacy and deepen your knowledge of each other in the way that God has provided.

 When you return from your honeymoon, you might like to ask yourselves and each other the following questions:

- What was the best sexual experience of the honeymoon?
- What was the worst sexual experience of the honeymoon?
- What is one sexual matter you would like your partner to think more about?

Finally, it is a profound part of the Christian view of sex that it is intended for procreation. Children are the ultimate expression of your 'one-fleshedness', carrying that two-become-one identity in their very bodies. Many marriage services include a specific prayer that God would bless the couple with children, and this is very appropriate. In marriage, a new family is being created. (It is a tragic loss for a couple when, for whatever reason, they cannot have the children they desire. Their grief is a common one, and it is deeply sad.)

The spark of desire we experience during puberty ignites in the sexual union of a married couple and then fans into flame in the gift of children. This exciting productivity is one of the marvels of our creator God, who ordered man and woman to be fruitful and to fill the earth.

Reading list

The following books are an assorted collection on some of the topics addressed in this book. Most are longer and more detailed than our introduction. Some of them come from non-Christian writers, and therefore do not espouse a Christian moral universe. We would not support everything that is written in each of these books. All the same, they are recommended for their helpful guidance on aspects of the topic.

Sex

Patricia Weerakoon, *The Best Sex for Life*, Apa Anglican Press Australia (Youthworks), Sydney, 2013. A guide to having a fulfilling sex life in the context of God's purpose for sexuality within marriage. Written by a Christian sexologist.

Douglas E Rosenau, *A Celebration of Sex: A guide to enjoying God's gift of married sexual pleasure*, Thomas Nelson, Nashville, 1994. An excellent guide to sex in marriage written by a Christian psychologist with around 20 years experience in sexual therapy.

Patricia Love and Jo Robinson, *Hot Monogamy: How to achieve a more intimate relationship with your partner*, Piatkus, London, 1998. Part workbook, part discussion, this is a very levelheaded approach to sexual behaviour in marriage, written from a non-Christian perspective but championing monogamy.

Rosie King, *Good Loving, Great Sex,* Random House, Sydney, 1997. A fun, informed exploration of how a good relationship and good sex go together. Very detailed but easy to read, written by a very popular Sydney-based non-Christian sex therapist.

Derek Llewellyn-Jones, *Everywoman: A gynaecological guide for life,* 9th edn, Penguin, London, 1998. The classic work on gynaecology, still excellent information for all women seeking to understand their own bodies.

Derek Llewellyn-Jones, *Every Man,* 4th edn, Oxford University Press, Oxford, 1999. The standard guide to men's health.

Judith K Balswick and Jack O Balswick, *Authentic Human Sexuality: An integrated Christian approach,* IVP, Downers Grove, 1999. A thoughtful and comprehensive overview of sexual issues from within a Christian framework.

Communication

Lawrence J Crabb Jr, *Understanding People: Why we long for relationship,* Zondervan, Grand Rapids, 1987. A biblically guided explanation of how people relate to each other and find their deepest identity in their relationship with Christ. More theoretical than practical.

Lawrence J Crabb Jr, *The Marriage Builder: A blueprint for couples and counsellors,* Zondervan, Grand Rapids, 1992. A very thoughtful and useful application of Crabb's psychological theory to building an intimate relationship with your marriage partner.

Deborah Tannen, *You Just Don't Understand: Women and men in conversation,* Random House, Sydney, 1990. A best-selling book by a professor of linguistics which describes the different expectations and approaches of men and women in conversation.

Homosexuality

Thomas E Schmidt, *Straight & Narrow? Compassion and clarity in the homosexuality debate,* IVP, Downers Grove, 1995. A detailed and careful discussion of the Bible's teaching on homosexuality as well as scientific and medical data concerning its possible causes.

Elizabeth R Moberly, *Homosexuality: A new Christian ethic,* James Clarke, Cambridge, 1983. A brief but powerful argument for what causes homosexuality.

Alan Medinger, *Growth into Manhood: Resuming the journey,* Shaw, Colorado Springs, 2000. A personal and practical exploration of what is involved in changing one's sexual orientation from homosexual to heterosexual.

In Australia, Liberty Christian Ministries offers information and support for Christians struggling with unwanted same sex attraction. Contact them by phone on (02) 9798 4685, or write to PO Box 67, Summer Hill NSW 2130.

matthiasmedia

Matthias Media is an evangelical publishing ministry that seeks to persuade all Christians of the truth of God's purposes in Jesus Christ as revealed in the Bible, and equip them with high-quality resources, so that by the work of the Holy Spirit they will:

- abandon their lives to the honour and service of Christ in daily holiness and decision-making
- pray constantly in Christ's name for the fruitfulness and growth of his gospel
- speak the Bible's life-changing word whenever and however they can—in the home, in the world and in the fellowship of his people.

Our resources range from Bible studies and books through to training courses, audio sermons and children's Sunday School material. To find out more, and to access samples and free downloads, visit our website:

www.matthiasmedia.com

How to buy our resources

1. Direct from us over the internet:
   - in the US: www.matthiasmedia.com
   - in Australia: www.matthiasmedia.com.au

2. Direct from us by phone: please visit our website for current phone contact information.

Register at our website for **free** regular email updates to receive information about the latest new resources, **exclusive special offers**, and free articles to help you grow in your Christian life and ministry.

3. Through a range of outlets in various parts of the world. Visit **www.matthiasmedia.com/contact** for details about recommended retailers in your part of the world.

4. Trade enquiries can be addressed to:
   - in the US and Canada: sales@matthiasmedia.com
   - in Australia and the rest of the world: sales@matthiasmedia.com.au

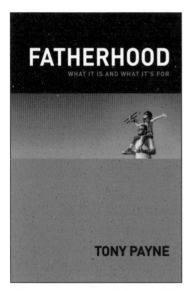